HUMANS ON THE RUN

HUMANS ON THE RUN

*of exiles
and asylum*

KUMAR M. TIKU

OXFORD
UNIVERSITY PRESS

OXFORD
UNIVERSITY PRESS

Oxford University Press is a department of the University of Oxford.
It furthers the University's objective of excellence in research, scholarship,
and education by publishing worldwide. Oxford is a registered trademark of
Oxford University Press in the UK and in certain other countries.

Published in India by
Oxford University Press
2/11 Ground Floor, Ansari Road, Daryaganj, New Delhi 110 002, India

© Oxford University Press 2018

The moral rights of the authors have been asserted.

First Edition published in 2018

ISBN-13 (print edition): 978-0-19-948481-2
ISBN-10 (print edition): 0-19-948481-3

ISBN-13 (eBook): 978-0-19-909530-8
ISBN-10 (eBook): 0-19-909530-2

Typeset in Arno Pro 10.5/14.5
by Tranistics Data Technologies, Kolkata 700 091
Printed in India by Replika Press Pvt. Ltd

Contents

CONTENTS

Prelude

Large swathes of Asia, the Middle East, and Africa are in the grip of religion, radical jihad, and an undying fealty to martyrdom. Where this will take us and how long it will be before violent political conflicts end are questions that no pundit would wager his money on. For years, conflicts have been the staple of the hourly news that we consume in print, on air, and online. The Twitterati and other inveterate instant messengers thrive on manufacturing dissent and mobilizing street anger. Somewhere in that space, every once in a while, we hear and see the homeless hordes. I belong to the multitude which comprises the conflict nomads of our times.

Well over a dozen countries today are steeped in race, class, and religious revolutions that, sooner or later, erupt in violent conflict, creating conditions for mass abandonment and homelessness, with millions forced to move multiple times within and outside their countries of origin in search of a semblance of peace, order, and stability. This book is not an attempt at making sense of the conflicts that have convulsed the world with increasing force, fury, and frequency, particularly in the last three decades or so. Nor does it strive to look behind the scenes for possible clues about international intrigues, and domestic class or power struggles.

This is a book of stories, pure and simple. In laying it out as it is, through a mosaic of mostly first-person accounts, the book provides clues into human lives that pass through the many and variegated tests of sustained conflict, migration, and multiple physical displacement. Through the stories, we begin to see the metamorphosis of once calm and orderly lives and the hard choices migrants face when they decide in favour of survival and self-preservation over threats to their lives, honour, and that most primeval of all human needs—freedom. We begin to see what happens to a person uprooted from the ecosystem called home.

The stories that you find in the pages that follow are an attempt at preserving memories of several microscopic journeys embarked upon by people, often under conditions of utter and complete hopelessness. In their own voice, individuals in flight, long disconnected from the certitudes of a settled, anchored existence, map their journeys when moving to the next village, town, city, country, or continent, in the hope of beating certain death, sustained denigration, and systemic abuse.

Serendipity, passion, and planning have all played a role in helping me listen to and narrate these stories. When I first felt the itch to make sense of conflict-scarred lives lived in perpetual homelessness, I had in my sights my own experience as an unrecognized, and not very recognizably displaced, Kashmiri person in India. For though forced into a lifetime of shaming homelessness, I was not living in a so-called 'camp', nor was I a recipient of the government dole, be that in the form of measly financial relief or any subsidized food stamps. Clearly, I did not fit into the archetype. Nevertheless, living amidst a family whose very existence in its years away from home was shaped and defined by the searing memories of sudden and forced migration during those dark and apocalyptic months in 1990, there indeed was material for not one but several stories from just my family alone. For thousands of Kashmiri Hindu families such as mine, the last quarter century has passed in juggling the demands of survival with the trauma of rejection and apathy that the community has faced in its splendid isolation as a castaway minority of a professedly secular republic.

My first United Nations (UN) assignment outside India took me to Afghanistan, where I spent just under five years, listening to myriad broken men and women who had lived to tell the stories of their shattered and scattered lives, and their constant search for a place safe enough to bring up their children. The stories that got to me more than others, I pursued to the very end, tailing those characters like a shadow through all their journeys, observing and processing changes in their psycho-social lives as perpetual journeymen with each setback and triumph. Some of those stories are a part of the collection in your hands.

Afghanistan was the first real pit stop en route to my ten-year-long professional journey through several conflict zones. Here, I made some lasting friendships with fellow UN travellers from conflict-affected Sri Lanka. I came face-to-face with Sri Lankan Tamil doctors and other aid workers who had harrowing tales to tell. I hope the two stories in this volume do justice to their remarkably resilient and textured lives.

Sudan was next. Depredations in Darfur, arising from differences among the Arab and non-Arab ethnicities, have left a whole people asunder and hundreds of thousands in a state of pitiful homelessness. By far, the bigger story during my time in Sudan was the impending referendum when the predominantly Christian South would take a call on staying with Sudan or having a country of their own. On 15 January 2011, the South Sudanese people spoke as one in favour of an independent nation.

I was there when Sudan split in two and the world's newest country, South Sudan, was born in the name of seemingly unreconciled religious and cultural differences. The euphoria of independence proved extremely short-lived. The lust for power among leaders of the two dominant ethnic strands of South Sudan, the Dinka and the Nuer tribes, has led to a civil war that has already claimed a heavy toll of life and forced millions to seek refuge in neighbouring Ethiopia, Kenya, and Uganda. Ethiopia, in particular, despite its own endemic poverty, has shown uncommon compassion and statesmanship in opening its borders to millions of people from more than one distressed country in its neighbourhood.

When I visited Ethiopia in the summer of 2015 to see first-hand this magic of a poor country with a rich humanitarian record, the streets of Addis Ababa were teeming with refugees not just from South Sudan, but also with people fleeing conflicts in Yemen, Eritrea, and the Congo. You will read about many of them in this book, as they speak about their current conditions and past lives.

After a second assignment in Afghanistan came the opportunity to serve the United Nations Children's Fund (UNICEF) in Syria. More than a third and close to half of the population here is without a home. The sheer scale of human tragedy that has visited this once beautiful and historically rich land is beyond all human imagination. For fifteen months, I travelled across the length and breadth of Syria as part of the UNICEF effort to deliver humanitarian aid—potable drinking water, basic supplemental nutrition, vaccination kits, school bags and textbooks, and medicines—to locals, many of whom were held in siege as human shields. I met and spent time with children and their parents in Damascus, Homs, Hama, and Aleppo, once neat and orderly cities that, for six years now, have been visited by war, bombs, and damnation, and resemble vast ruins. I met countless mothers of the hapless children in these cities who were living in refugee camps and unfinished buildings, trying to soothe the frayed nerves of their little ones and stay sane in the face of relentless, heavy bombardments, and, of course, getting used to a life of perpetual migration, from one neighbour-hood to the next, often one city to the next, and in so many cases, one country to the next. Small wonder then that Jordan, Lebanon, and Turkey host close to half the Syrian population between them today.

In the northern part of Iraq, in the valley of the Dohuk governorate that falls in the historically charged semi-autonomous region of Iraqi Kurdistan, I chanced upon camps upon camps of the Yazidi community. A small religious minority with its own distinct cultural practices and way of life, the Yazidis mostly inhabit the area of Mount Sinjar of Nineveh province. Radical extremists that had declared a caliphate from Mosul in Iraq to Al-Raqqa in northern Syria (and which now is close to unravelling, what with major Iraqi advances in Mosul and more determined air and land effort to beat the group into submission in Syria) made Yazidis their early prey, committing unspeakable atrocities and hounding them out of their habitat and forcing themselves upon countless Yazidi women. The savagery that this beleaguered minority has endured has been captured on prime-time global news shows and in the press. Accompanied by Sarwa Qadir, a highly sensitive Kurdish colleague, I sat down with one middle-aged Yazidi woman to make sense of her life and experiences at the hands of the terrorists and her journey to a refugee camp, as a young, vulnerable woman, mother of a small brood of children, and homemaker.

What motivated those journeys made by people across multiple geographies, cultures, and time zones? What kind of memories of a place that an individual calls 'home' refuse to disappear and define the idea of identity long after the person was forced to abandon it? And what is at the heart of the undying and near-universal yearning to 'go back' to the place that is home—a metaphysical counterpoint to the daily ravages and indignities of forced nomadic life of sorts?

The stories, covering a wide cross-section of humanity and nearly every part of the world in conflict, attempt to answer those questions. Together, the stories paint a picture of the human as a homeless creature on the run. The stories largely conform to a template of storytelling that I designed at the start of this documentation project. For places and case studies that I could not directly visit, I relied on some brave and exceptionally gifted storytellers. These fellow collaborators in this project agreed to follow my story template and contribute their original writings for this collection.

The tapestry of individual voices within the pages of this book shines the spotlight on migrant lives, encompassing a mélange of human experiences through multiple migrations, experiences that range from the tragic to the sublime, with many shades of grey in between. When all options for safe survival are exhausted within their own homes, people move to the next neighbourhood, then the next proximate village, town, or city, and as we have seen with alarming frequency in South Asia, the Middle East, and Africa, to the next country that holds out a promise of calming the storm in their lives, the storm borne of brutal, barbaric, violent events that threaten to rip apart nation-states and their social fabric built over a millennia and more of settled existence.

In my neck of the woods, by the time the last Soviet soldier pulled out of Afghanistan in February 1989, over 3 million Afghan men, women, and children had come to make peace with a refugee life, mostly in Pakistan and Iran, with all its attendant deprivations and indignities. The refugees were followers of the same religion, inhabitants of the same land, and raised in its manifold blessings, separated and cleaved by a conflict that fed on ethnic differences among the various stocks of people that comprise the great rugged landmass of Afghanistan.

Egged on by their respective allies in the Muslim world, the Pashtun, the Tajik, the Hazara, the Uzbek, the Aimak, and the Turkmen Afghans unleashed a civil war on each other and their land of birth; it went on for decades, resulting in the most monumental population displacement in history at the time. Young boys of all ethnicities were given to war as fat to fire. The seemingly never-ending wave of slash-and-burn methods has taken the country back to an age of anarchy and left most of its public infrastructure pillaged and destroyed. Not a single family in Afghanistan, whatever its ethnicity, has been untouched by the brutality of war.

The war has trundled on, albeit with added ferocity and different methods and objectives. Children continue to pay the price in terms of a stolen childhood. Reconciliation projects, gently initiated by the international community, have for the most part been dead on arrival. Lack of trust in each other and in the state in Afghanistan is as apparent today as it was when I first set foot on its soil a decade ago.

Kashmir, the conflict-affected part of the state of Jammu and Kashmir in India, was to follow Afghanistan in its manic urge for self-destruction. By 1990, an uprising, violent in its methods and decidedly communal in its tone and tenor, had convulsed the length and breadth of Kashmir. The state and civilian authorities, missing in action at the best of times, capitulated as the frenzy overtook the street. *Azadi*, the stock-in-trade of the largely educated and jobless youth who led the loose, rag-tag guerilla movement for change, seemed just a push and a heave away. The movement targeted flags and other totems of state authority, unfurling its own flags in busy market squares. This was accompanied by targeted killings in cold blood of prominent persons from the minority Kashmiri Pandit community. The killings met with their intended objective as fear, cold and unspoken, ran through the relatively minuscule community. As local media reported on the killings, the question in every Pandit home was, who next?

Anyone who has been a minority of any form or typology would know well how fear breeds panic. One by one, in the dead of the cold winter nights, the Pandit families left their homes in a panicked rush. What was at stake was not just the life, limb, and liberty of the men but also the honour of their women. I belong to the Kashmiri Pandit community whose origins in Kashmir date back to several millennia before the advent of Islam in the Valley. Mine was among the nearly hundred thousand families that caved in to the fear and somehow made it to the safer, though many times more uncertain and unfamiliar, parts of India. This book of stories stems from my own tattered identity as a Kashmiri.

Among the first crop of boys to initiate a paradigmatic shift in civil resistance in Kashmir was Ashfaq Majeed Wani, a fearless young soul oozing bravado. Wani was only 21 when he was picked by Syed Mohammed Yusuf Shah, the Pakistan-based chief of Hizb-ul-Mujahideen, to be his polling agent in the 1987 elections to the Jammu and Kashmir state assembly. The elections were said to have been blatantly rigged, as Shah, now better known as Syed Salahudeen (ostensibly after the 12th-century first sultan of Syria and Egypt who led a military campaign against the crusader states in the Levant) found himself on the losing side against a leading light of the then ruling dispensation. Soon thereafter, young Wani decided to take to armed methods to vacate purported Indian misrule in Kashmir. In leading a crusade of sorts, Wani was asserting his right to a home that was undefiled by the hands of what he perceived as an 'external' occupier.

A leading light of militancy in Kashmir, Wani was a year junior to me in college in the early 1980s. I knew him up close as a rakish young teen often surrounded by slightly brazen teenyboppers who were never above making a racket in the college canteen and were usually spoiling for a fight with fellow baddies on the campus. In my term as the president of the students' union at the Gandhi Memorial College in downtown Srinagar, on more than one occasion, I had to use my traction with the college management to have a rustication memo against Wani annulled. We became close and even joined forces as one team to compete in an inter-college athletics event held in the University of Kashmir, where à la Milkha Singh, he ran barefoot and won the race hands down.

In time, Wani found his machismo, athleticism, and fearlessness getting harnessed for the cause of liberating Kashmir from the so-called occupation by India. His naturally subversive instincts, always in full display during our college days, became the stock-in-trade of the militant creed as he took on the mantle of the Jammu and Kashmir Liberation Front (JKLF), the first among the pro-independence insurgency movements that caught popular imagination in the early 1990s in Kashmir. He galvanized large sections of Kashmiri youth for the cause of azadi. A symbol of freedom and courage for the younger generation, his daring attacks received fulsome coverage in the Srinagar-based Urdu media. Local legend had it that Wani had crossed over to Pakistan and returned fully trained in the use of small firearms and motivated to lead an armed struggle for independence of Kashmir from India. He was part of the dreaded HAJY quartet of the JKLF that also comprised Hamid Shaikh, Javed Nalka, and Yasin Malik. Ashfaq Majeed Wani was killed by security forces in March 1990, at the age of 23. Millions turned up on the streets of Srinagar to eulogize him and mourn his death.

Two-and-a-half decades later, Burhan Muzaffar Wani, another young Kashmiri boy from the rural outbacks of the southern part of Kashmir valley who embraced the militant cult, captured the imagination of the world, as his namesake predecessor had done. His death at the hands of the security forces became a nonpareil symbol of popular resistance in Kashmir. Burhan Wani rose to be a leading light of the pro-Pakistan militant organization Hizbul Mujahideen. A product of his times, he harnessed social media to the hilt to re-unify the new generation of Kashmiri youth in its civil resistance methods against the Indian state. A common thread that ran through these two lives was their uncommon youthful zeal and a pious determination to lead the march of Kashmiris from perceived Indian oppression into an idyll of freedom and dignity. Even as thousands of young lives have been snuffed out in the violence in Kashmir over the years, these boys were among just a handful to receive public adulation of such magnitude.

This book is a compendium of human displacement caused by conflicts in the last 25 years or so. These have been the years during which I have moved from being a man with a home to an uprooted, upended, home-less person of the world. During these years, I have grown from being a young, green, and full-of-beans individual to a grey, middle-aged person, displaced, dispossessed, and weary from the daily gripes of dystopia. This book has mined a sliver of that memory from many different parts of the globe where conflicts have boiled over and resulted in a mega-scale movement of ordinary citizens, living a once-normal life, to conditions of progressive dehumanization.

This has been a time during which I have raised a family and sired a child who, at 23 years of age, is a made-in-Delhi, second-generation-homeless adult, blissfully disconnected from her roots, the same rootlessness that is a source of abiding helplessness for her anguished parents. Disconnected from home and its essential moorings, they often wonder aloud about how their daughter and future generations of this exiled tribe might describe themselves in the years and generations to follow.

The loss of the land into which my forebears and I were born is a stab whose pain refuses to be dulled even after a full quarter century in displacement. During all these years, our dinner-table discourse has unfailingly centred around how it was back home, and inevitably led to opening each night the gnawing wounds of memory as the mind reels back into that shaming experience of being kicked out of my own home by frenzied zealots who implemented with clinical precision the project of setting man against man, and splicing our shared land and heritage.

The Constitution of India, that ultimate arbiter of my destiny as the citizen of a free, secular, and democratic republic, in that part of the country at that point in history, stood like a mute witness to the forces of division, unable to stop the rage and fury of a mass hysteria of separation that was in the air, much less, able to show the light towards a future of mutual coexistence. So many years on, what has changed?

Home was not just the house that I grew up in or the street that I played on. Nor the hills that stood like silent sentinels, watching over my beautiful vale and its inhabitants in almost divine care. Nor the scintillating and many-splendoured lakes, springs, and rivers and their calming waters that would flow by unhurried, but sustained the whole ecosystem and imbued the Kashmiri character with a certain composure and a poetic heart. Nor even the majestic chinars that had for ages embalmed innocent lovers and lent leafy shade to travellers and vagrants alike.

Home was not any one of those attributes of the space called Kashmir. Home was the person that I became when these elements came together to shape and make me. Away from Kashmir, my home, I mourn the loss of that person inside that deserted me bit by bit as survival and adaptation in distant lands and alien cultures took centre stage. Now while the conscious self may have moved on, as indeed may be the case with the Kashmir of my youth, the home that I left behind, the search for an elusive habitat that I can truly call home continues to shape my dreams even after a full score and seven years in exile.

While the days are spent in the lethal grind of humanitarian jobs, some of which took me to the most conflict-ridden hotspots of the world, the nights have almost perennially been occupied by a decidedly different landscape. My nights are consumed with dreams of the land I was banished from, for no reason other than being on the wrong side of the religious and political divide. The impact on my senses has been at once calming and unsettling as I battle the juxtapositions of a daily life in displacement with my nightly life in a calming, imaginary homeland. It is a barely concealed psychological disturbance that's perhaps a fit case for some much-needed psycho-social help.

The émigrés, who accounted for but a minuscule 3 per cent of the population of the Kashmir Valley that is predominantly populated by the Sunni Muslims, testify to succumbing to fear triggered by a handful of targeted and spectacular killings, and radical intimidation in the form of incendiary communal slogans emanating from mosques, particularly so in neighbourhoods with Hindu presence.

In the city of Srinagar, for centuries we lived in clenched proximity with our Muslim neighbours across countless localities. Vichar Nag, Raina Wari, Sathu Barbarshah, Nai Sadak, Badyar, Habba Kadal, Bana Mohalla, Chinkral Mohalla, Fateh Kadal, Ali Kadal, Nawa Kadal, Safa Kadal, Chatta Bal, Kak Sarai, Karan Nagar, Bal Garden, Jawahar Nagar, Raj Bagh, Indira Nagar, and Shiv Pora were some of the neighbourhoods in Srinagar that the Pandits inhabited in visible and, in some cases, sizeable numbers.

In those three brutal months of 1990, however, these neighbourhoods were emptied of their presence almost completely. The killings of a handful of notable members of the community in the Valley, among them an elderly judge and a senior political party worker of the Bharatiya Janata Party—a leading political party that is in power in India since the 2014 Lok Sabha elections, and a partner in the current governing dispensation in the state of Jammu and Kashmir—and a notable youth worker, had already hit the mark in injecting a deep sense of uncertainty, fear, and a sense of 'who next?' among the minuscule Pandit community.

The killings were complemented by a targeted campaign by the ideologically driven toughies that made use of the loudspeakers in the neighbourhood mosques—the same amplifiers that the muezzin used to call the faithful to prayer—for blaring out manifestly provocative slogans calling upon Hindus to participate in the project of ushering in Nizam-e-Mustafa (the rule of Allah). It is instructive and no less ironic to recall that even in those heady days of azadi—a sentiment that professedly represents the pure desire for liberation of Kashmir at once from the clutches of India and the embrace of Pakistan—the movement fell back on religious bigotry to advance their message among the masses.

This became a regular feature of those cold winter months. As the 'loudspeaker threats' grew in force and frequency, they served their intended purpose in sowing a deep sense of fear among the Pandits across all 10 districts that make the Kashmir part of the state of Jammu and Kashmir. Unable to cope with the sweeping radicalization of the Muslim mind and a rising crescendo of secessionism that had taken over the Kashmir Valley, in a matter of months, Kashmir witnessed the exodus of the Pandits from their homes across the Valley.

The scale of intimidation targeting the Pandits recalled the depredations unleashed by Sultan Sikandar Butshikan, the seventh Muslim ruler of Kashmir, by most historical accounts a rabid iconoclast who ruled in the late 14th century and presided over the massive desecration of Hindu temples in Kashmir. The ruler is known to have ordered mass conversion of the Pandits to Islam as well as caused large-scale migration of the Pandits to the plains of the northern mainland of India.

Just imagine: the Pandits who represent the warp and weft of a distinct tapestry of the life of Kashmir were scared out of their wits and forced to run away to safety while their neighbours and their countrymen alike merely looked on, or simply looked away. The Kashmiri Pandits—with no Kashmir for a home any more—in a bit of a hyperbole, use words like exodus and ethnic cleansing to draw attention to the wholesale forced flight from their homes and centuries-old habitat. Today, barring an odd family that bucked the tide of migration, the Pandits are practically written off from the Valley. With no real initiatives of genuine reconciliation forthcoming, their prospect of returning to their home seems bleaker than ever.

The Muslims among whom I was born and raised are among the finest specimens of the human species. We drank from the same rivers and shared a social camaraderie and togetherness that only the uniquely syncretic culture of Kashmir could nurture. The best that can be said about the perceived Muslim betrayal of the Pandits in the days leading to their mass flight out of Kashmir was that the ordinary Muslim approved of the militant creed almost willingly, to express, as it were, his strong disenchantment with a prolonged period of inept 'elected' rule that, in effect, was a travesty of good governance in every way.

For the motivated young militants of the time, turning the tables on Delhi, the Indian capital that is perceived in Kashmir as the seat of all intrigue, meant support for 'independence' from the puppet rule in the state, even if that came with the price of dispensing with the Pandit community that was integral to the Kashmiri way of life. The seeds of an Islamic enclave within the borders of a secular republic were well and truly sown. Twenty-seven years went by in a trice, without anyone so much as noticing either the flight of a whole people or indeed the progressive communalization of a political conflict. In this time, Pandit homes got pillaged, torched, or sold, and bit-by-bit all traces of the Pandit way of life in Kashmir became nothing more than a memory.

After several false starts and stops trying to find our moorings in Jammu, the nearest town that promised a respite from the haunting fear of terrorism that had overtaken my valley, we dropped anchor on the outskirts of Delhi, an ever-expansive city of hope, opportunity, and freedom, where work was easier to come by, and with the perspective that only time and distance provide, memories of fear and the flight from our homes in Kashmir would hurt less, giving way to the cut and thrust of everyday existence of an average metropolitan life.

In the fullness of time, my work with the UN took me to some of the conflict hotspots of our times that grabbed global attention—Afghanistan, Sudan, Syria, and Iraq. I spent a decade of my life in these countries, my ear to the ground, making sense of the lives of people who had experienced and survived the many ravages of displacement and lived through several false starts to their lives that often never got going. Millions of forced migrants around the globe nurture the very same dream that I dream—of returning to their home one day, when injustice, violence, and terror will give way to reason, sobriety, and fair play. For many the dream never materialized. Others returned from years of escape and exile only to find ashes where once their homes stood. Through those years in the field, I stood witness to the depths of human misery, impoverishment, and helplessness, but also to countless stories of resilience, triumph, and hope against all odds.

Back in the winter of 2014, during my visit to Aleppo in northern Syria as an aid worker, I visited a large shelter hosting children and families displaced by the ongoing conflict. The conversations turned inevitably to their worries about winter. Like young Ibrahim, who I met in a temporary shelter in western Aleppo, hundreds of thousands of conflict-affected children and families in Syria were bracing themselves for the descent into freezing winter temperatures. With more than 6.4 million people—including 3 million children—displaced from their homes at the time, many lived in temporary shelters that could provide scant protection from the cold and limited heating and availability of hot water for bathing.

Often these shelters were no more than open, unfinished buildings, without doors or windows, and sometimes lacking even external walls. Families made do with polythene sheets to cover holes and stave off icy winds. Up to eight people would be squeezed into one or two rooms. In the northern regions of Syria, temperatures regularly plummet to sub-zero levels, exposing children to the risk of respiratory infections and other communicable diseases. With health services in the country stretched to the limits, the risk for sick children of being left unattended during the long winter months was present and clear.

Approximately 4,000 families were living in the shelter I visited in western Aleppo and many were already beginning to experience the harsh realities of winter. With night temperatures having dropped appreciably across northern Syria, these families were ill-prepared to protect their children from falling sick—or worse. Most families, having migrated from the eastern side of the city, were in desperate economic straits and coping with the worst living conditions imaginable.

One family living in an incomplete building whose sides were open to the elements were dreading what lay ahead.

'This winter is going to be unimaginable,' said Monaf, a father of three children aged between 7 and 11. 'I shudder to think how my children will survive this winter.'

Lina, who lives with her three children at the shelter I visited, had limited means to prepare for the winter ahead: 'Being prepared means winter clothes for my children, warm bedding, and heating in the house,' she said. 'This is how we used to prepare before the war forced us to leave our homes. As a single mother, and without work, I cannot afford to look after the needs of my children. I worry all the time if my children will survive this winter.'

In Afghanistan, over a five-year horizon, I travelled across a dozen provinces and made connections with returnees making sense of their existence and contemplating the future of their children with a gnawing sense of concern and hopelessness as war raged on in the country. In the world's youngest nation, South Sudan, I saw how a people that fought for and won their freedom from the Muslim-majority Sudan found their dreams turned to dust as power-hungry satraps of the newly independent country stoked ethnic fires that resulted in an epic displacement of the newly free citizens who have now run away in droves to neighbouring Uganda, Kenya, and Ethiopia. A calamitous famine has made a tragic situation worse and a continuing civil war in the country borders on genocide.

In place after place, I became aware of how the triple whammy of a travesty of justice, severe exploitation, and terrorism of one kind or another leaves ordinary people with no option but to move. The familiar scenario of the sway of radicalized armed thugs, either from shadowy militant organizations or belonging to the state machinery, got repeated in different places. People got displaced, moved back, and then moved all over again. In the harshest of settings imaginable for survival, children and women survived—often by selling their bodies or through labour— in the absence of male members who were either consumed by conflict, passed from this world way before their time, or were enlisted in their countries' armies. Sustained threats of physical assault hastened the movement of people in most cases. Weak and failing states largely stood by without being able to make a material positive difference to the lives of their displaced and abandoned citizens and state subjects.

The stories birthed by conflicts and forcible displacement are too vast and too many to be packed into one book. As conflicts grow in numbers, force, and intensity, so does homelessness.

What you now hold in your hands or see on your screens is a book of stories by people done in by wars and protracted conflicts. Taken together, the stories should help us understand what it means and takes for a person to be on the run and live and still hope for elusive calm and peace when war comes to our land, increasingly without notice.

In speaking to me and my fellow contributors, a total of 25 exiles, refugees, and asylum seekers across more than 10 countries have opened up and shared a sliver of their lives. Each story is a microcosm of the gargantuan homelessness and displacement challenge of the country that the person represents.

As you soldier on through the pages of this book, it is my hope that the stories will leave you richer in understanding the experience of homelessness and stronger in your resolve to be a part of the solution.

Because, as the cliché goes, tomorrow might be too late.

AFGHANISTAN

'Afghanistan—where empires go to die.'

Mike Malloy

Afghanistan is a landlocked country in Central Asia, which shares borders with Iran, Pakistan, China, Tajikistan, Uzbekistan, and Turkmenistan.

Afghanistan's population, according to recent estimates, is over 36 million. Some 42 per cent of Afghans are Pashtun and 27 per cent are Tajik. Hazaras and Uzbeks each account for 9 per cent of the population.

There are two national languages: Pashto and Dari. Pashto is the language of the Pashtuns and is spoken exclusively in many parts of the south and east. Dari, a Persian language, is spoken mainly in the north and central regions of Afghanistan.

Only around 38 per cent of Afghans are literate.

Afghanistan has suffered from such chronic instability and conflict during its modern history that its economy and infrastructure are in ruins, and many of its people are refugees.

Dreams Are Dreams

She walked into my office at the United Nations Development Programme (UNDP) one August morning in Kabul in 2007. She introduced herself as a communications staff at a large project on conflict prevention that was supported by UNDP. I was still new to Afghanistan, still getting used to the stark contrasts in freedoms on offer for men and women. She had a spark in her eyes, a spring in her step, and a natural ebullience that I could barely associate with the archetype of Afghan women that I had come to accept as de rigueur—coy, unfailingly withdrawn, with an almost sly and self-conscious way of walking in public places that spoke of an ingrained fear of being seen in public, legacy of the dark Taliban rule. Hasina wore a headscarf and seemed totally in tune with the prevailing mores of Afghanistan in the tonality of her expression. She surveyed the three men and two women in my office who comprised my team, and offered her greetings in a warm but restrained manner. I was the last to be greeted, of course, with a dose of the fulsome love for India that springs from every heart in Afghanistan. Ice broken, we got down to the business of working out the support that she could look forward to receiving for a commemoration event of her project that dealt with the Disbandment of Illegally Armed Groups. That first meeting set the foundation for a close friendship that has endured over the years.

Gazing at the Afghan carpet in the living room of my Austrian abode otherwise furnished with European fittings, breathing in the interlaced aromas of Kabuli pulao and that typical smell of novelty that new homes come with, and listening to my children segue seamlessly from German to Pashto, I realize that as a girl, crouched in her basement out of fear, I would have never dreamt of this life.

Homelessness is a word that has become synonymous with conflicts. As an Afghan woman who was greeted with the rumblings of war and conflict as soon as she was born, I have since found myself in a perpetual state of displacement. Yet, not once have I wanted to be out of my own country for good. I just cannot imagine myself to be out of Afghanistan for long.

As a child, there was hardly a day when fear left my heart as shells and rockets flew all over the neighbourhood all the time. It was almost a dream to go to school without fear. The 1990s saw the civil war in Afghanistan reach a crescendo. Kabul resembled a battleground that was taken over by armed groups. Living in a downtown neighbourhood, I remember my siblings and I finding ourselves captive in the basement of our home for hours and days together. It is perhaps not without reason that most traditional homes had a basement to stock up on household supplies and for families to retreat into in times of danger. The sound of shelling and gunfire was all around us.

I grew up in a big house with a nice garden. In summer, the garden bloomed with greens and fruits but we were almost never allowed to play there, since some of the fighting groups were firing away at enemy positions literally from behind our house. We grew up deprived. But never hopeless.

Even through those days of growing up in the shadow of death and constant fear, it was Plar Jaan (father) who was our beacon of hope and source of all support. My four sisters, two brothers, and I always looked up to him for words of courage. He instilled hope in us. He said everything would be fine and one day very soon the dark clouds of conflict and sounds of rockets would go away for good and peace would return to our lives. Years passed, we all grew up, but peace never really returned.

Coming from a military background, Plar Jaan was adept at packing us off into various safe havens within the house and protecting us from the shelling. We were split into groups in a way that ensured that in case of a rocket attack on the house, at least some of the family members could survive.

During long spells of violence those days, we wasted months together waiting for the fighting to stop and for our schools to reopen. With no chance to venture into the streets, the basement of our house would turn into a makeshift school on most days. When the situation in Kabul became somewhat better, the schools re-opened. The main school had been burnt down in the fighting so the girls' school was started in a makeshift government building in the centre of Kabul. In those days, there was no proper furniture. It wasn't unusual to spend an entire day in school standing as there were never enough benches to sit on. The classrooms were always overcrowded and chaotic, but we were happy that we at least had this opportunity to go to school after having been confined to our homes for almost two years.

By the late 1990s, the Taliban had arrived in Kabul. For ordinary citizens of Kabul, life took a turn for the worse. The Taliban wasted no time in foisting their dark ideology on the citizens. They reserved their worst excesses for girls and women. They were going after anyone and everyone who had been associated with the regime of the ex-president, Dr Najibullah, who they considered to be an apostate.

My father was a high-ranking defence official of the Afghan government during the Najibullah era. It was natural that sooner or later the Taliban would come looking for him and arrest him. Until the Taliban came to power and enforced their radical ideology with an iron hand, Plar Jaan never considered the option of fleeing from Afghanistan, even though millions of my countrymen had already crossed into Pakistan to escape the war. But once the conflict moved from the fighting for ascendancy among various Mujahideen groups to the enforcement of ideologies of the radical-minded Taliban, he wasted no time to announce that the family should leave for Pakistan at once.

It is true that with the arrival of the Taliban the security situation had improved a great deal. The daily violence on the streets of Kabul had receded. However, the Taliban had imposed so many restrictions on the daily lives of people that there was fear all around. It seemed that wherever one looked, it was as if human beings were mere soul-less bodies.

Finally, in 1998, I left a sad, dusty, and scared Kabul behind and arrived in Peshawar, a city that struck me as many times greener than Kabul and full of flowers. Once there, I experienced freedom. For me, as a teenager, that meant being able to go to school without fear, going for a picnic with the family, going to the neighbourhood park with friends, and watching TV without the fear of being captured by the Taliban. Altogether, for Afghan refugees, life was hardly much easier than back home, but at the time nothing seemed more precious than freeing ourselves from the daily excesses of extremism that had been perpetuated in my homeland.

It is never easy to abandon one's home and start living in another country, but for me it was an experience to remember and learn from. The political situation in Pakistan and Afghanistan has been unstable for decades, yet ordinary people have learnt to live through the most difficult challenges. Through our darkest days, we never lost sight of sharing our love and respect for our fellow citizens. I remember the grace, love, and sympathy of our Pakistani hosts and neighbours. They made it easier to adapt to the new reality of a refugee life.

It was in Pakistan that I took my baby steps towards connecting with the outside world by taking my first lessons in English and computer studies. Soon, my younger sisters and brothers got the chance to go to school. My father and my elder sisters found work as teachers, and life seemed to feel normal again. I was selected as an English teacher in the institute where I was studying.

What makes Pakistan more special for me is that I met my life-partner there, through some common family members, and soon we got married. Around the same time, the early 2000s were turning into a special time for the people of Afghanistan. The Taliban were being driven out of Afghanistan and a new government under the leadership of Hamid Karzai was taking control. Once that happened, we returned to our country. But it was different for me this time—I was coming back not with my parents and family, but with my husband and in-laws.

The whole world extended its full support to the reconstruction and development of the country, and after years of suffocation and suffering, there was hope on the horizon that the women of Afghanistan would have it good again. Thousands of new jobs were on offer for the educated young generation.

I was fortunate to find a job as a communications assistant with one of the international organizations based in Kabul and earn a distance learning diploma in journalism from one of the leading institutes from London. Life was getting better day by day, and we were hopeful that our dream of a peaceful Afghanistan was coming true. However, dreams are dreams. They disappear from our sight even before we know it.

The experience of working in an international organization taught me so many things. It gave me the confidence that as a woman I could work alongside men and contribute as much as them—an idea that had till date been foreign in my universe. My work experience taught me how to fight and win the battle for my rights.

In spite of the overwhelming support of the international community, those in charge of so many of the vital institutions of the state were the same people who were involved in the large-scale destruction of Afghanistan in the 1990s. The government largely, if not predominantly, comprised elements that had spent years fighting each other and seizing control of major parts of Kabul. The only difference was that while in the 1990s they were fighting each other with guns, now that they were part of the same government, they were busy propping up criminals, indulging in large-scale corruption and even narcotics smuggling. Even though there was a sovereign and elected government in place, not much was being done to rid the country of violent armed groups and there was a sense of growing insecurity among ordinary citizens. We had quickly earned the dubious distinction of being described as one of the most corrupt countries in the world with the highest incidents of violent crime.

As time passed, and with each year, the dream of freedom, stability, and a life free of insecurity was beginning to turn sour as violence in the form of a resurgent Taliban reared its ugly head. Once again a new phase of insecurity began, and by and by, all the problems of before came back to haunt us. My biggest disappointment was the ever-so-slow progress on giving women the space, freedom, and opportunity to express themselves through their talent. In the initial years following my return to Afghanistan in 2001, I felt more empowered as a working woman. The strong presence of the international community meant that the conservative elements in the government could be kept under check. However, with the passage of time and as the government wrested control of more and more institutions, demanding a vastly reduced international footprint in matters of governance, I experienced a perceptible shift backwards in the attitude of my male colleagues towards women's work. Women who had reached higher levels by virtue of their hard work and abilities were especially targeted and singled out for discrimination. It was, once again, a case of one step forward and two steps back.

I witnessed discrimination from close quarters. The international organization that I was a part of handed over the management of its peace-building work to an empowered national institution that many of my colleagues and I were given the opportunity to work for. In the interests of securing our jobs as much as being of service to our fledgling nation, many of us opted to work for the national government. I witnessed a sea change in the organizational culture as I found myself at the receiving end of distorted male attitudes, regular blandishments, and brazen discrimination in distribution of work responsibilities. All too suddenly, the framework of respect towards women that I had come to expect for nearly 10 years of my working with the United Nations (UN) seemed like a thing of the past.

By now I was the mother of two kids. When I first started working, I had promised myself to work for my country and seize every opportunity to be of some benefit to women. I was mentally prepared to sacrifice my life and freedom in return for being an active participant in the reconstruction of Afghanistan. But when it came to my two sons, I was getting increasingly concerned about their safety and their prospects in a country that was fully in the grip of insecurity, lawlessness, and monumental corruption.

I roughed it out as a working woman in Afghanistan for over a decade. Looking at the future of my children, I could see only uncertainty all around us. After a lot of thought, my husband and I resolved to initiate steps to move out of Afghanistan again in 2012, this time to Europe, a continent that promised fairness and decent prospects for my children.

The only realistic way out of Afghanistan was through touts and agents who operate in the business of human trafficking. I would never have imagined that such a tribe of people could exist. They were two steps ahead of the law and helped desperate asylum seekers reach their destinations without a hitch. Once I became aware of such 'operatives', I soon found out that there was a well-established system of human trafficking in place, one that Afghans had been making use of for years.

The process seemed reasonably simple. With great reluctance and fear in my heart, I decided to seize this opportunity and trust the services of an agent to get me and my family out of Afghanistan. The agent asked for a few photos and a hefty fee—that set us back by a lifetime of savings—to be paid once the client was safely ensconced in the country of asylum. It was difficult not to take my parents and other close members of the family in confidence. But I was ready. I put all my hard-earned savings at stake and even took a loan so my family and I could be ensured safe passage out of Kabul to a country that promised us peace and safety.

Having heard several heartbreaking stories about human trafficking and the fate that awaited asylum seekers, I was fearful and apprehensive.

Some had even paid with their lives or been separated for long durations from their families. In my case, however, it all worked out surprisingly smoothly and we entered Europe in 2013 without facing any major problem on the way.

This trip brought me face to face with the reach of human smugglers. I discovered, to my amazement, that these people are always several paces ahead of the government and the organizations that are working to prevent human trafficking. They are well informed about every border and coach asylum seekers on the various steps of the journey—where to do what and how to talk if confronted by difficult immigration authorities. Our destinies were tied to Austria with no consultation or consent from us. We could be in any other part of the world and have led completely different lifestyles had it been for a different human trafficker. Sometimes I wonder how these little contingencies have the capability of changing the course of one's life.

As an asylum seeker in Austria, life in those initial months was anything but easy. All manner of adjustments in lifestyle are needed when one is assigned to live in a camp. Getting used to our ration of pre-cooked Austrian food was difficult. Not being able to converse in German proved a major handicap. There is also a natural though implicit hostility among some locals towards 'outsiders'. I met so many fellow refugees who, after their arrival in Europe, had gone into a state of deep depression.

But for all that, we were only too relieved to be in a place that was so completely at peace—something that my husband and I had almost forgotten and my two little children had perhaps never experienced. Before long, I found odd jobs as a translator with some immigration lawyers—an experience that eventually helped me to compete and make the cut for the job of a refugee coordinator with Caritas, an international non-profit organization dealing with refugees. Securing this job has been a major success that has come my way since migrating here, second only to the positive judgement on my asylum application by the Austrian authorities. I would be helping refugees coming from different countries build their initial understanding of the prevailing laws and entitlements governing refugee integration in Austria.

In the media, we always hear about the problems that asylum seekers encounter on the way to the countries where they go to seek refuge. There is hardly any discussion about the psycho-social trauma and issues of loss and maladjustment that so many experience in their new settings. Seamless migration to a new country demands quick adaptation, but no matter how prepared one is to blend in and embrace the new culture, there are enough impediments along the way. It took a long time before I could be confirmed for a language course. Then again, I found the class mixed, where beginners were lumped together with those that came from high academic backgrounds, leading to inefficiencies in the learning process.

But none of this mattered to me once I found the system so completely responsive to the needs of my children. From the time they arrive in Europe, refugee children must go to school. The system is fully geared to help integrate children into the new environment.

For me personally, it was a difficult transition as I'd had a great job back in my country and suddenly found myself in the role of a housewife. But I was happy for my kids—they were safe and busy with their school. Having done well with the German language course, I am now more satisfied with my progress in this new environment. Being able to speak German, although hardly fluently, I am able to make new friends and contacts every day and reach out to new people. After three long years of struggles and daily lessons and learning in a new country, I can say that I am well on my way to feeling integrated with my adopted society.

Self-belief is what has brought me this far in life. I survived many tough tests in Afghanistan and Pakistan. I am in a good place now and have every intention to be an active member of this society and to serve my people, one way or another. Living in Austria, I want to continue my education and raise my kids in a good way to be great Austrian citizens and hopefully be of use to their motherland one day. As an Afghan woman, completing higher education was a dream, away and out of reach. But dreams are dreams. They have a way of coming true.

Hasina is not her real name. She chose not to be identified for reasons of personal safety and that of her family.

In Wilderness, I Lit a Lamp of Light Called School

I was born and raised in a well-to-do family in Kabul, the historic and once grand city of Afghanistan, known in the 1960s and early 1970s for its pristine promenades and a liberal culture that was the envy of the region. Growing up in the lap of nature amidst the peace and quiet of those days, I had never imagined that one day I would end up a refugee in a pretty wretched part of Pakistan.

I must have been 10 when my father, an engineer, was posted to the southern city of Kandahar and the family moved with him. The year was 1975. My father, Mohammad Asif, was assigned to the Meteorological Department of Kandahar airport. My siblings and I were soon admitted to a school that specially catered to the children of employees working with the civil aviation ministry and was conveniently located inside the airport. Those were the days when Afghan children benefitted from state-sponsored compulsory education. I completed high school there and later took history and geography as my main electives for my 12th-grade graduation from the same school.

Back then, those in government employment were a privileged lot. I was raised among well-educated, upper-middle-class families that populated the housing colony around the Kandahar airport area. For a number of years, four to be precise, life inside the compound went on smoothly. The first signs of unrest in our lives surfaced in the wake of the Soviet occupation of Afghanistan in 1979 and the armed resistance that the invasion engendered in parts of the country. Conflict became a part of our daily existence in the 1980s. We somehow kept out of harm's way as city after city got sucked into the vortex of violence.

In 1987, after my marriage to Sher Muhammad, a government employee, we moved to Kabul where my husband was posted. I started my career as a Dari language teacher in a local school. Happily married to a loving man, successfully pursuing my passion for teaching, and still young—those were the best days of my life. Kabul in those days seemed a relatively safe place to be. Alas, those joy-filled days were not to last for too long. The insurgency that had been developing across Afghanistan in response to the Soviet occupation had started to engulf Kabul as well. Then, when the Mujahideen ousted the Communist regime, complete chaos erupted all around the capital.

Fear and revenge was in the air. Everyone and anyone associated with the Communist government was a marked person. Being a government employee and seeing too many of his associates either perish or disappear without a trace, my husband spent restless nights fearing for his own life and that of his family. As fighting amongst various ethnic groups intensified, one day, we decided that time had come to leave the country to a place of relative safety—just like so many we knew had done before us for similar reasons.

In 1992, taking only a change or two of clothes each, we left with our two children, aged three and four. It was a time when almost everyone we knew seemed to be on the run, keen to get out of harm's way by leaving Afghanistan. In that haste and in the chaos all around us, I could not even grab a moment to see my parents for one last time since they were living some distance away from us, in a different locality. I was somehow able to meet my brother who urged us to leave the country without any delay.

A long and hazardous journey ensued and we finally found ourselves in Mianwali, a rather remote town in the Punjab province of Pakistan.

Before long, we settled in a refugee camp named Kot Chandna, situated on the outskirts of Mianwali. Far away from the cheer and joy of my cherished classrooms of Kabul, I was now face-to-face with the harsh reality of life in a tribal refugee settlement where poverty and cultural sensitivities conspired to keep children, particularly girls, out of school. As for boys, in those dire economic conditions that communities faced in the camps, parents elected to send them to work instead of schools.

The UN refugee agency had opened five schools for girls in Kot Chandna in the early 1980s, but the conservative refugee elders disapproved of education for girls. For a good 10 years before we arrived in the area, the school buildings had remained devoid of girls. It was in those refugee camps and in this setting that I restarted my teaching career 26 years ago in Pakistan.

One of the lessons I learned early on was that in order to smoothen the way of children's education in an economically desperate and a men-first social setting, I had to first educate the parents about the importance of letting their children, especially their daughters, go to school. Having been raised and married into progressive families, I knew the value and power of education.

Now, as I stepped into an area of obscurantist impulses, this was the moment of reckoning. I needed to carve my own way. I knew in my heart that with persistence and perseverance, I could add meaning to my refugee existence by lighting a lamp of education among young children whose entire childhood was in clear danger of being frittered away in darkness, illiteracy, and unknowing.

And so it was that I embarked on a long journey of combating the stereotypes surrounding girls' education that were festering in the camps and taking root in an environment of growing want and helplessness. I took it upon myself to don two hats—one of a teacher and the other of an agent of change working to smash barriers and open closed and puritanical minds. It was a tough challenge. My deference to prevailing customs and traditions, and a non-confrontational approach towards the elders helped me gradually work on the minds of even the most conservative members of the refugee camp. Through all of this, the support of my husband was invaluable.

He stood beside me like a rock and gave me the confidence to work with courage and determination to bring about even a semblance of attitudinal change in a milieu seeped in the dead weight of extreme conservative orthodoxy that was designed to steal women's freedoms and future security as homemakers and fellow contributors to our society.

I would go door-to-door in Kot Chandna, sitting with sceptical parents and persuading them to send their daughters to learn the basics of reading, writing, and arithmetic. With discussions and sessions that stretched over days, I struggled initially to convince even 20 parents about the real value of education for their children's future.

Of course, my clear offer to parents was to send their children to my school in the camp. I literally stood as surety for the safety and well-being of these children. As refugees, dealing with extreme limitations of space was our first constraint. We had to make do in a single room in a house owned by my husband's brother. I borrowed a tent to teach the refugee girls whose parents I had managed to convince.

In those initial years, I gave my students handwritten copies of textbooks because I could not afford to get printed ones for the whole class. I had no other option but to write my own book incorporating different subjects for the students. I would spend my days teaching and looking after my family and my nights writing these books.

Making them literate was one undertaking, but I also wanted to introduce them to personal hygiene and a minimally healthy lifestyle that was possible even in the desperate sanitary and environmental conditions in these resettlement areas for Afghan refugees. In the initial weeks of our classes, I taught my students about the importance of cleanliness, social behaviour, how to dress, how to use shampoo and soap, and the importance of washing and changing clothes at frequent intervals. Teaching such basic life skills was of paramount importance in the camp where people in general led desperate lives.

To keep a balance between education and local traditions where girls are expected to get married and serve their in-laws, I also started introducing girls to home management skills, such as serving guests and how to excel at home cooking. I introduced them to different recipes and lessons about presenting food to guests. By and by, I found they would practise my lessons at home and apply the skills in their daily chores.

In a matter of months, the number of students climbed from 20 to 60. As word spread about the benefits of giving girls a shot at basic education, more and more children from nearby areas started to attend my half-way school.

Two years later, in 1994, a local NGO happened to visit our camp. Seeing my passion and vision for girls' education, the NGO offered support. That help meant that for the first time since my school was set up, I was able to distribute proper stationery and books among my students. I was beside myself with joy when I got books, pencils, erasers, and other items. While distributing the stationery, I observed some of the students had started biting at the eraser, thinking it was chewing gum. They would often say, 'The colour is good but the taste is sour.' It just showed what a novelty even the most basic tools of schooling were for the refugee children whose parents in general must have enjoyed much better days, both at home and in school, back in their days in Afghanistan.

The NGO started paying me a token monthly salary of 1,200 Pakistani rupees (USD 12). The funding was short-term and stopped after a year. Meanwhile, I continued to persuade local parents to send their children to my school, and enrolment figures kept on increasing, albeit slowly. This was a time when both my husband and I had to regularly make do with little or no income. But I never gave up, and my perseverance paid off when the office of the UN High Commissioner for Refugees (UNHCR) took note of my work and showed interest in supporting me in my endeavours. It provided me with five tents and I taught in them for two years. By then, more and more refugee elders had started to recognize the value of education and my work. Soon, the number of students soared into hundreds.

Having started in 1992 with only one tent and 20 girl students, today my school caters to the schooling needs of hundreds of Afghan refugee and local children from nearby areas. A total of 136 Afghan refugee girls are currently enrolled. More than 1,000 Afghan refugee students have completed their studies till date. Many of my students have repatriated to

Afghanistan and are serving their country, playing their little part in the reconstruction of their motherland. Why, some are even paying back to society by spreading my legacy. For instance, one of my female students, upon her return to Afghanistan, set up a home-based school for girls in Kunduz to reach out to local families and provide access to education for those returnees who were unable to attend formal schools due to cultural sensitivities and social norms.

Through such students, my work gained wings and its scope extended over the borders back to my home country. Empowered and educated returnees who share my vision continue my work and contribute to the reintegration of their returning compatriots as well as to the broader reconstruction and nation-building processes in Afghanistan.

With my modest efforts and respect for prevailing customs, I managed to bring a small change in the mindset of a section of the conservative Pashtun population, without challenging their core approach to living. My approach enabled me to gain respect from the community that I had set out to work with and change.

Ten years after I started my work with children in my self-run schools, the UNHCR proceeded to negotiate with the local community to reopen its schools, which had remained effectively unutilized thanks to strong resistance from the community elders to modern education in general. Sensitized over the years by the positive impact of my self-run school, this time the elders agreed without objections.

I am currently teaching at one of the government-run girls' schools. The Government of Pakistan's Commissionerate for Afghan Refugees appointed me on a starting salary of 2,800 Pakistani rupees (USD 28). Now, my salary stands at 10,000 Pakistani rupees (USD 100) per month, which has enabled me to support my husband and six children. My husband runs a small grocery shop in the refugee village, and together we strive hard to keep the wheel of life rolling.

When I arrived in the camp in 1992, life in Pakistan as a refugee was one long ordeal. On the one hand, I was dealing with the trauma of separating from my family, and on the other, I was juggling to adjust in the new surroundings of a refugee camp. I lost contact with my loved ones.

For almost three years, I had no clue whether my parents were still alive. Back then, there was no mobile phone facility available and hardly any way of keeping in touch. The residents of the camp were friendly and hospitable. However, their restricted lifestyle and conservative approach towards women troubled me no end.

In such an environment, I could either go with the flow and be lost in the religious and cultural orthodoxies or I could risk taking small, audacious steps towards changing the mindset of people aligned for centuries to old beliefs and ideologies of ignorance. I thank my stars that I made the choices that ultimately lit a spark of hope in so many homes, but more importantly, promised a better future for the discriminated and despised girl children of the refugee camps.

I witnessed the most painful experiences of my life when I arrived in Pakistan as a refugee. In the protected surroundings of Kabul and Kandahar, I had never realized that a large segment of Afghans was still following the centuries-old practices of barring women from decision-making and treating them in an unequal manner. For the first time in my life, I was meeting women for whom the concept of a female teacher was akin to a character in fairy-tales.

Once inside the camp, we were shown to our room by my husband's friend who had made arrangements for us. I stepped into a very dark and small room. Nothing was intact and in order, as if this camp too was affected by war, like Afghanistan. The room felt like an underground dungeon. It was so dark and despondent that I wondered if the war had also reached this part of Pakistan. Later on, I realized that this was how refugees in the camp lived; it was a lifestyle inflicted upon them by poverty, lack of education, and no exposure to the outside world. The majority of the camp residents in Kot Chandna were Kuchis (nomads) who were used to a vagrant lifestyle.

When women from nearby houses came to see me, I was surprised and shocked to see them as much as they were to see me. Their hair, as a rule, was unwashed and uncombed and hence tightly tangled into filthy dreadlocks. Their sweating faces and crumpled and crushed clothes told stories of the toil and privations of their tender lives. I could not believe that these people were from my own country.

To see so many of the girls from the camp educated, to know that they can read, write, and type SMS messages on their mobile devices, and even use the Internet, fills me with boundless joy and hope for their future.

My students have gained their in-laws' respect due to their education. Most of the village women often come to me and tell me that every boy wants to marry a girl who has completed her education from this school. I think this is a big step forward and a far cry from the time when boys could not countenance the idea of being married to educated girls or the fact that girls had been to school.

Being a mother of six, I have worked hard to provide a decent education to my own children. I spend almost my entire salary to pay the tuition fee for my son, Sameer Ahmed, who moved back to Afghanistan and now studies engineering at Kabul University. However, I cannot afford to send my daughters for higher education. My hope is that one day, my school, which is currently a secondary school (from first to eighth grade), will be upgraded to a high school so that my students, and my daughters, can study further. My second son, Mohammad Waseem, is studying in high school, and my youngest daughter, Sawera, is a bright young student in fifth grade.

Three years after fleeing Kabul with my husband, and losing all contact with my siblings and parents, my brothers tracked me down and visited me in the camp. Six months after that, my parents came to see me. They were rather distraught to see me, their pampered princess, living in near penury, with no house of her own, a borrowed room, and a jobless husband.

But I also sensed a tinge of pride in them upon seeing me take charge of a hopeless situation and bring hope to other children by spreading the joy of education. Today, all my siblings are back in Afghanistan and serving their country. There are doctors and teachers in the family serving their countrymen in different parts of Afghanistan.

I have taught thousands of students, many of whom have gone on to play an important role in their communities in both Pakistan and Afghanistan in different fields. I feel content with what I have done. Perhaps God sent me to Pakistan to educate these children.

Over twenty years ago, I planted five trees in the courtyard of the compound where I first set up my tented school. Every day I look at these trees, which have borne witness to my struggle. These trees grew with my students. They personify my students, who are now living fruitful lives.

I am happy. I have no regrets and I have done something I am proud of. The tasteless erasers brought fragrance and colours to the lives of these girls.

POSTSCRIPT

An Undelivered Letter

Letter to an Azadi Radio programme called Sabiqa Qaharmanan (Stories of Heroes) on the story of transformative change in the lives of Afghan women who started in the refugee camps of Pakistan in Kot Chandna.

From Halima, Karishma, Bibi Jamila, and Sharifa, graduates of eighth grade from the batches of 2004 and 2005.

We would like to offer our deepest gratitude and admiration to you. Your engrossing program has struck a chord of interest with us and we would like to unveil an astonishing and historic fact of life. We belong to a society where girls are kept aloof from the social sphere and confined to their homes, where education for girls remains a distant dream and is considered a deadly sin.

Our story is the story of Afghan women.

More than 20 years ago, we were living with our families in the lap of the mountains of Kunduz, Takhar, and Badakhshan. In 1982, like the rest of our compatriots, we too lost our livelihoods and fled for our lives. From being a family of sheep and cattle herders, we became refugees in a huge Afghan camp called Camp Kot Chandna in the Mianwali district of Punjab, some 300 km away from the cities of Peshawar and Lahore. We began to live in this camp located, much like our home in Afghanistan, on the cusp of a mountain.

The UN, donor countries, and Jihadist organizations took measures to help the refugees. A school was opened there so that boys and girls from the camp could study. Most families, however, did not appreciate their girls going to school. Since the charity organizations did not wish to offend the cultural sensitivities of the refugees, they kept the educational services restricted to a limited number of children.

The girls could only watch their brothers attending school. As girls, they were expected to be content living a life of illiterates, like their mothers and grandmothers had done. Schooling was only for boys, almost by right. The girls could not even imagine getting education because it was thought that women did not have to think about anything other than serving the men of the family, cook, clean and produce offspring.

Meanwhile, around 1988, it was rumoured that the UNHCR was planning to open a girls' school in the camp which was predominantly inhabited by the Kuchi community of animal herders from the provinces of Kunduz, Baghlan, Samangan, Logar, Jalalabad, and Paktia. This elicited an agitated response from the elders across the length and breadth of the camp. The long dark night we were living through as girls did not see the light and sun even as late as 1992. It was April 1992 when the Communist regime fell. It was good news. Everyone started thinking about moving back but then we learnt that the country had slid into an even more vicious war.

A man, who was a relative, who had moved to Kabul in good times in search of better opportunities and had ended up marrying a teacher, joined the wave of Afghan refugees in Mianwali who had escaped the flames of the new war. Since he was related to one of us by blood, he came to seek refuge in the camp. This newly arrived family was welcomed by Malak Sahib who gave him a room next to his place.

The respected teacher was the focus of amazement and I thought it was strange that even such urban women had to spend their lives in such a barren and downcast refugee camp when they were forced to. To cut it short, the teacher attracted the attention of my family. She became popular in the neighbourhood. The popularity of the Kabuli teacher was a matter of pride for us. She requested the Malak, an influential Baloch personality in the camp, to let her use her room as a classroom for the first grade and to use a part of the mosque for the girls.

Malak Sahib thought deeply about this, especially about girls' education. In the end he allowed it with a condition: that the teaching would only be religious. He also told her that if any girl behaved in a non-serious manner, she needed to let him know. This way the teacher invited 15–20 girls to her room and, using her experience, she started teaching us. We would take one-hour lessons with great interest every day. I being quick on the uptake, it did not take the teacher long to shower her special interest in teaching me. It was as if the sun had finally started showering its light upon our village.

For several years, the teacher continued to teach us by putting in her time and meagre resources in making learning fun for us. It was probably 1994 or 1995 when a woman from an NGO visited the camp and was pleasantly surprised to come across a woman running a course where the number of students was above 40. She spoke with our teacher and then sent us books for grades 1, 2, and 3, as well as blackboards and chalks. She also gave 1,200 Pakistani rupees to our teacher. We were making progress in our learning and seeing it. Our families were happy with us; they had changed. I suppose it was the end of 1996 when the UNHCR got to know about a miraculous educational course for girls in the camp. A sympathetic official named Naeem Durrani came to the camp to see the course.

He praised our teacher and then spoke to Malak Sahib to seek his approval for turning the course into a formal school. Malak Sahib put forth certain conditions and then agreed. On 12 December 1996, girls of my tribe became part of a school for the first time ever. The school was built in five tents. With the new funding, we got plenty of educational material and now there was even a fixed salary for the respected teacher. Thus the school attained its own unique identity. Since it was associated with the family of Malak Agha Mohammad, no one dared to object. Seeing this, people in other parts of the camp were also inspired and allowed the UNHCR to build schools.

Slowly the number of schools reached five, and 1,700 girls were enrolled in these schools. Currently, there are four schools up to fifth grade, and our school, which is up to eighth grade, continues to provide quality education to refugee students. So far, three classes of eighth grade have graduated from our school. Girls are finally receiving the light of knowledge at these schools.

We have plans to become teachers once we return to Afghanistan. Our teacher is teaching at the middle school number 2 now. We hope this letter would be broadcast. However, we would not like the name of our hero to be announced on the radio.

The letter about an unsung hero couldn't be delivered and hence was never broadcast, but it is a source of encouragement for the teacher. Whenever she feels dejected, she reads the letter, which inspires her and bolsters her strength and commitment.

—As told to Qaiser Khan Afridi

ERITREA

'Ana sabr heliko ask sabr abieni.'
('I'm still patient until patience gets tired of me.')

Alamin Abdulatif

Young people are fleeing the North African country of Eritrea due to 'open-ended' national service, soaring food prices, paucity of clean drinking water, and poor job prospects.

Eritreans constitute a major chunk of those arriving on the European shores by sea. According to the European Asylum Support Office, 47,020 Eritreans applied for asylum to European Union countries in 2015 and 38,808 applied in 2016.

All I Wanted Was to Play Football

I had just finished meeting the head of the Jesuit Refugee Service (JRS), an international faith-based humanitarian organization in Addis Ababa, capital of Ethiopia. Among a sea of women and little girls who had assembled at the small JRS compound for a verification exercise of their refugee bonafides and to collect their fair share of rations of rice and cooking oil, I saw Amanuel, a lone man roaming about with a slightly lost look. Middle-aged with a slim frame, there was desperation obvious in his fidgety gait as he frantically went about enquiring from the volunteers and staff about the time when the ration counters would open. I took him to the side and introduced myself vaguely as a chronicler of refugee stories. He was more than keen to talk. I offered to take him out of the compound for a short drive around town and perhaps a meal together, but of course only after he had dealt with the more urgent business of collecting his rations. Amanuel was an unlikely Eritrean refugee to be found in Ethiopia. Ethiopia and Eritrea have been bitter enemies that fought a two-year war from 1998 to 2000 over a border dispute. The war claimed tens of thousands of lives and rendered thousands more homeless in two of the world's poorest countries. Despite several attempts at arbitration, extreme bitterness and covert conflict continues, largely spurred by cross-border intelligence operatives on both sides. Then, what was Amanuel, an Eritrean national, doing in an 'enemy' state? Read on.

As an Ethiopian by birth, and Eritrean by nationality, I am a strange animal: neither trusted by Eritrea nor wanted by Ethiopia. I have been on the run for years. Still, I wait in hope that one day, in the not-so-distant future, I will discover a place that welcomes me without suspicion. Every tomorrow brings new hope, so who knows, I may find myself in a good place one day.

I was born in 1974 in the Lideta suburb of Addis Ababa. It was the same year that the Marxists in Ethiopia staged a coup to overthrow Emperor Haile Selassie. I was the youngest among my eight siblings. Even though my fellow Eritreans had waged a civil war of independence against Ethiopia in the early 1960s, the Ethiopian–Eritrean military conflict was far, far away from anyone's imagination. Eritrea has coexisted with Ethiopia as a part of it for millennia. It was still one land and one country when I was born and growing up.

I completed my high school education at Bole High School in the Ethiopian capital. Football had become my passion right from the time I was a young student. It still is. I played the game as a mid-fielder, and played it well. I joined the Youth Ethiopian Football Club and on the side also represented a famous football club affiliated to a bank in Addis Ababa. My family backed me in my decision to play and gave me their full support. I must say though that their focus was on providing me the best education possible. My brothers Jones and Azeb guided me towards becoming a good student. A national football federation member who was in charge of training women helped me a great deal. The club coach and one of Ethiopia's famous body-builders were my role models. Together with a friend of that time who played for the Police Club, they were be my heroes and I looked up to them throughout my youth.

After school, the only two passions that I nurtured were music and football. Higher education is for sissies, I felt. It is all about rote learning, not for creative and energetic people. Once I finished high school, my father helped me set up a small store for general supplies. Later I worked with a tea manufacturing company and went on to work as a guard. I served as a guard for one year in a private security company.

Eritrea was liberated from Ethiopia in 1991. In 1998, when armed conflict erupted again between the two neighbours, Eritreans in Ethiopia and other neighbouring countries were forced by the liberation fighters to move to Eritrea. Having lived all my life in Addis Ababa, I was suddenly made aware of my Eritrean nationality. I had little choice but to head north to Asmara, the capital of Eritrea.

I was among the tens of thousands of youth who were forcibly conscripted for military service. Upon completion of my initial training, which lasted a year-and-a-half, I was assigned to the special commando brigade, led by Colonel Salu Usman. Soon, I was chosen for a more intensive eight-month-long military training in advanced weaponry systems. I was recruited in the military in the capacity of a soldier, without any rank or title, at a salary of 250 Eritrean nakfa (about USD 25) a month, and sent to the battle frontlines in Chad. After yet another round of training in automatic weapons and new defence systems, I was picked to be a part of the covert Eritrean operations to destabilize Ethiopia by training the rebel Somalian and Ethiopian opposition groups.

One of the groups that I trained was called the Tigrayan People's Liberation Front. My role was to help redeploy new weapons that reached the military centre in Asmara among the Ethiopian rebels on the borders. Often the weapons would come via the black market from Libya and were usually delivered by sea.

The state authorities in Eritrea were no less than any terror groups. Being of a communist dispensation, religion was an anathema to them.

A soldier without vices was suspect in the eyes of the officers. Often, to escape harassment at the hands of my seniors, I would feign being drunk most of the time. Since excessive drinking was the norm, it was safe to have a slur in your speech and not sound like you are sober and sensible when everyone else is having a hard time standing erect. Once, I was even jailed on charges of covertly working for a humanitarian charity that belonged to a Christian missionary group.

There was a military coup d'état mounted by Colonel Usman. The government tried to quell the coup and ended up arresting everyone close to the colonel. I escaped punishment because, sensing the trouble to come, I had crossed over to Kasala in eastern Sudan, in the desert area between Eritrea and Sudan.

One of my uncles had been living in Kasala for over 40 years. For more than five months, I took refuge with him. From there I went to Khartoum, the Sudanese capital. My uncle helped me prepare travel documents that would help me live and work there. While in Khartoum, my plan was to make arrangements to migrate to Libya, but the fragile security situation in the country forced me to change my mind and I went to the Ethiopian embassy in Khartoum instead to apply for refugee status. That is how I returned to Ethiopia, this time as an urban refugee. It has been nearly a year-and-a-half since I arrived, but that seems irrelevant since I have not received any refugee assistance in Addis Ababa till date. I am on the brink of penury and desperation.

The Eritrean spies are all over Addis Ababa. Because of my past history of serving in the Eritrean military, I fear for my life all the time. The law does not allow refugees to seek formal employment in Ethiopia. Surviving without work and money in living conditions that are anything but human, I pass my days in a state of utter destitution, forever in wait of the generosity of fellow human beings.

My background in sport has lent me the resilience that I needed to survive the harsh odds in my life. On the odd occasion when a relative in a distant land sends me a bit of money as a living allowance, I spend it on drinking. Other than that, I have no vices. I am not into women. For one, if you are as chronically depressed as I am, you lose your drive for sex.

Besides, having a woman is my life means taking on additional responsibility. I have no money for that.

The best years of my life were when I was still an adolescent in Ethiopia. I had just passed out from the high school. Things were good in the family. It was perhaps the only phase of life when I had access to fresh food. I wore clean clothes. That was the time when I was also enjoying football. I used to go visit stadiums to watch my favourite club play. We used to drink draught beer, dance, and make merry when our teams won. Life was good. I didn't have a job but used to get regular pocket money from my family. Often I would jump the walls of the stadium to watch the matches and avoid paying for the ticket. I even made money by selling invalid and obsolete tickets from earlier matches to football-crazy fans. That's how I used to cheat to make a quick buck to entertain friends.

I have never been married, but I was in a long, serious relationship with a woman during my time in Eritrea. This was because I never earned enough money to have a wedding. We loved each other dearly. In the three years that we were together, she went through three abortions as she suffered from gynaecological complications. We sought the help of traditional healers due to our inability to pay for hospital bills. But nothing worked. I couldn't help us.

It has been over two years since I fled Eritrea. I have no information about my girlfriend and her whereabouts. She used to work as a maid in someone's house and had a brother who used to help her. It was heartbreaking to leave her behind, but those were very traumatic times when I was running for my life all the time. Neither of us had the money to pay for the broker to show her the way out of the country. Also, she did not participate in the mandatory national service, which made it all the more difficult for her to leave. She did not have even the right to seek employment in a government office. This was despite the fact that she was a high-school graduate.

If I stay here in Ethiopia, I have no hope left for survival. My only hope is to receive the UNHCR's assistance and find an opportunity to resettle in a European country. Several of my relatives have moved to Italy and the US, but no one has come forward to help me, either financially or through sponsorship efforts. These days, I am surviving on a ration of rice and cooking oil from the JRS in Addis. For accommodation, I keep moving from one place to another but basically I have no address and no home to call my own. I rely on the generosity of my friends to keep me in their homes.

I cannot afford house rent. I only have money to get through this day. Is this how the world should deal with a high-school graduate who once played football and simply wanted a decent life?

INDIA

'One individual may die for an idea, but that idea will, after his death, incarnate itself in a thousand lives.'

Subhas Chandra Bose

The Internal Displacement Monitoring Centre (IDMC) estimates that there are at least 796,000 people internally displaced as a result of conflict and violence in India, as of 2016.

Based on its monitoring, the IDMC believes that at least 448,000 were newly displaced in 2016 by conflict and violence. Displacements occured mainly in the states of Assam, Nagaland, and Jammu and Kashmir.

Following communal violence in December 2014 in the districts of Chirang, Kokrajhar, Sonitpur, and Udalguri of the western part of the state of Assam, up to 300,000 people took shelter in 91 relief camps. It is estimated that around 1 million people were displaced by similar spates of communal violence between 1996 and 2013. For some, the events at the end of 2014 led to their second or third displacement.

There are 60,500 Kashmiri families registered as internally displaced people (IDPs) since 1990. This amounts to 350,600 people as calculated by the national family size average of 5.8 people according to the 2011 National Census. Of this total, 38,100 families reside in Jammu, 19,300 families reside in Delhi, and the remaining are in other states. In addition, cross-border tensions with Pakistan displaced an additional 20,000 in October 2014 and a further 10,000 in December 2014/January 2015.

Maybe the Birds Are Homeless Too

My sweetheart and life partner, Sudha, has a story that is every bit as compelling as any you will read in this compilation. Seeing me take off for multiple journeys to meet people of multiple nationalities, she one day sat me down in our pigeonhole home in Noida, India, to know more about the nature of my current exertions and if she could justifiably qualify as a case study to be included in the collection of displacement stories that I was busily putting together. No stranger to her life and her many tribulations from an early age, I grudgingly agreed, with the caveat that the final call on whether the story would make it to the book would depend entirely on the merit of the content. Hers is one of the two stories from the 1990 migration of Kashmiri Hindus, which saw Kashmir nearly cleansed of the minority community, bringing an end with it to a cosmopolitan multicultural fabric of the state that has been sundered before but has somehow survived for the better part of the last three centuries.

I am off for the day from my office in Connaught Place in central Delhi and I am heading, with brisk steps if I may add, towards my home in Habba Kadal in downtown Srinagar. With brisk steps. It is early evening in winter and I must reach home before it is pitch dark. I walk through the narrow, long, serpentine alleys of Srinagar. I come across familiar faces from familiar surroundings in familiar attires. Others too who I encounter on the streets are rushing back home as if to avoid being caught in the cross hairs of an untoward incident. There is tension in the air. My shoulder unwittingly bumps against someone going the opposite way and I wake up to a warm, humid morning in Delhi. Upon opening my eyes, I realize that this is the same dream that has been haunting me for all the years that I have been in Delhi, away from my home in Srinagar.

The dream repeats itself, with minor variations in locations. Sometimes I start from Nehru Place in Delhi and have to reach Fateh Kadal in Srinagar, and on other occasions I start from Noida and have to reach Lal Chowk. In each of these dreams, my home is somewhere in Srinagar and my workplace in Delhi. The fact, though, is that I left my home in Srinagar behind a long time ago.

I have been living away from my home, in forced exile, for the last 25 years. I have built a nest just outside Delhi, but in my dreams, this is clearly not home. Home is where I was born and brought up, a place that belonged to me and cradled me, from my birth through infancy, then adolescence and early adulthood. Home for me means Srinagar, the town that connects me with my identity, my heritage, and my ancestors.

Never ever have I been able to find the same sense of belonging in this part of the world. My life in a metropolitan city is a complete antithesis of my small-town origins. My existence is as faceless here as it was intimate back home. I look around expectantly for signs and shades of my early life. From moving out of the hills to the plains, life has changed—and how!

Home is where the land is circled on all sides by peaks that stand like sentinels in their resplendent majesty, dressed in beautiful white all through the long and dreary winters, leaving one feeling cozy and secure in a heavenly citadel. Where the azure sky on most days of the year is ravishing in its transparent blue, the clouds thick and cottony white carpets in the sky. The sun always shines so tenderly warm, its steel rays falling on the snowy peaks and lifting one's spirits even in its afterglow... The rains always arrive on time and, falling on the tin roofs, make for divine music. When it snows—God, how it snows in my valley!—it is as if Peace herself in her white garb descends from the heavens. Where the birds chirp the sweetest of melodies and the bumblebees hum to the tunes of freedom. Where the river flows quietly and watches lives full of energy and innocence flourish on its banks. Where the lakes in the heart of the city, calm and poised, reveal yet another visage of heaven on earth. Where beauty, innocence, and contentment define life everywhere and love springs from the depths of the soul and where care and concern for others reigns supreme. These are some crystal-clear memories of my childhood that refuse to dim, let alone die after all these years in exile.

In school and college, we worked hard to stay on top of our studies, and even stay ahead, but it never seemed like the cut-throat race to the bottom of human relationships that is almost the norm in the big city. If one made it in life with toil and sweat, there was no rush to exponentially increase one's possessions. Happiness was found in taking a long journey inwards, hand-held by saints and seers who we would go looking for in distant ravines and villages where they lay in communion with the Almighty.

I cannot forget waking up to the ringing of bells from Hindu temples and the *azaan* in the nearby mosque, almost in unison. The shrines belonging to Hindus and Muslims stood cheek-by-jowl and I remember my grandfather teaching me to bow my head in reverence and quiet contemplation at the door of every mosque. Everyone belonged together and stood by each other in every sphere of life. All through those childhood days, the evening ritual was to watch the birds flying away in flocks. My grandmother would often say these birds were heading home after attending their school. Their loud chirping, she said, was akin to the loud noise that we would break into upon hearing the final long toll of the school bell that would denote the end of the school day. How I loved to witness that sight every evening!

And then one day, out of the blue, it all changed. Some straws in the wind, if one was able to catch them, spoke of change in the air, but it was still somewhat under the surface. Or perhaps we lay in denial, refusing to accept the fact that things were not quite the same any more. Friends and neighbours from the majority community, whose presence we had grown used to and would rely on through good times and bad, started becoming distant and impersonal.

A strange silence engulfed the whole atmosphere. Killings which were unheard of in my homeland became the talk of the day, every day. No one quite understood who was killing whom, and why. For the new creed of trigger-happy zealots, anyone and everyone dubbed as an informer had to pay with his or her life. In the venomous bazaar of trading secrets, a *mukhbir* (informer) was the one who would be sentenced to death without a hearing. This new nomenclature was unheard of before in common parlance. At the same time, it became a norm to switch on the news on radio and TV and hear about crackdowns and military actions in the far outback of the Valley where militant insurrectionists were being hunted out without mercy. Violence begets more violence, just as love begets love. The virtuous wheel of love and inter-communal bonhomie in the Kashmir of my birth and the exemplary peaceful land of my forefathers was being quickly overtaken by a vicious cycle of distance, distrust, and destruction.

I was barely getting used to the constricting new reality of living as a minority when one day a friend lost her mother in cross-firing in the city. When I went to commiserate, I was shocked to find this friend holding back from giving full expression to her grief of losing her mother in the increasingly violent city of Srinagar. She just did not want to talk about this great loss in the family and chose instead to maintain a strange stony silence, ostensibly to preclude the possibility of the mourners breaking into loud sobs. There were no words of sympathy coming from them nor was there any anger against the perpetrators.

I began to realize the gulf that was beginning to appear between two communities that had peacefully coexisted for centuries. The feeling of being shunned and silenced by fear sent a shiver down my spine. How could my Muslim neighbours and friends be so callous as not to allow, let alone join in, mourning this untimely death? Something that would have been par for the course in the not-so-distant past in the Kashmir that I knew and grew up in.

There was fear everywhere, and mourning the premature and infinitely sad loss of a noble woman and a fellow communitarian was no longer an occasion for expression of genuine sympathy. It was clear—there was something holding back the communities from grieving together. Was it fear, or something else? I had no clue, but I was filled with shame and disgust that my friend was left stifled and unable to even mourn her mother's death.

Even with all that was going on in the vale of Kashmir, not the wisest amongst us could have wagered a bet those days that we would be so consumed by fear, very soon, virtually the whole community would leave behind their homes and their hearth, and hundreds of thousands of people would cross the very mountains that had kept them secure, in search for a safe refuge on the other side of the Jawahar Tunnel.

The talk back then among the migrants was that the frenzy would die out soon and the locals, our brothers-in-arms, would come back to their senses and stand surety for our safety as they had always done in the past, before the Valley erupted in a sudden and seemingly new convulsion of targeted killings of local Hindus. The wave of violence that fed on radical Islamist slogans was completely alien to the composite ethos of the Kashmir that I had been born and raised in.

As rumours of a coming Armageddon that would finish off the Pandits swept through the Valley, I sat huddled with my teenage brother and my mother, together trying to make sense of what was happening around us, and mapping our next steps. Loudspeakers from many a mosque blared chilling slogans of incitement, calling upon the Hindu men 'to leave the valley with dispatch but leave their women behind for they were needed by the Muslim men to increase the *ummah*'. When the slogans reached our ears, my mother was shaken at the thought of our future. It was just the three of us in our family, my father having passed away at a young age. We understood that we could not stay a moment longer without inviting an unknown, unspoken catastrophe, and finally we decided to bid adieu to our home and run to safety in the great unknown of Jammu, the nearest Hindu town, which we would otherwise frequent for occasional trips to escape the extreme winters of Kashmir. Like most people who were hurrying out of their homes, almost in their pyjamas, we left too in the dead of the night, hoping to return as soon as a semblance of order was restored. We left with heavy hearts, knowing we were leaving behind not just our sparse worldly belongings, but our very base, our roots, our entire ethos, as we headed out to a space of seeming safety and not much else.

Who would have dreamt that as we left our homes, our next-door Muslim neighbours would say little beyond a perfunctory 'Khuda Hafiz', and not stop us with all their resolve from going away, from being uprooted. Little did we think at that time that we would never return to our homes, nor ever be seriously implored to stay, or return, by our fellow Kashmiri Muslims who, in a different era, would have given their lives to stop the extremist madness that was taking root in the Valley.

The course of my life changed forever on that dark night when I left with my brother and mother along with an aunt's family in a truck that was hired to take us to Jammu. The night was eerie. Everyone was sad but no one knew that the journey would take them away from their homeland never to go back. No one was talking. There was complete silence throughout the journey. At dawn, we reached our first port of call in displacement, my maternal grandfather's house. It served as a base camp for many families, and from here started the journey of our struggle to strive and forge ahead, against all odds.

Jammu is where I started the journey of getting into a mental state of lost identity, but it was the older generation that was the worst hit. Dislocated and destitute, they found it impossible to cope with the ignominy of homelessness. The harsh tropical weather of the plains was a far cry from the salubrious days in the Kashmiri homes that they once inhabited.

In contrast, in the migrants' camps on the outskirts of Jammu, young girls and women were particularly hit by the sudden loss of privacy and the abysmal state of public hygiene. Snake bites and heat strokes felled many among the elderly, as medical bills soared and incomes shrank. Life in tents and one-room tenements proved almost too harsh to bear for the proud and hitherto-sheltered Pandits.

There were hardly any psycho-social support services at hand, in the camps and our temporary homes with the host communities, to help children cope with the scars of war and displacement. Almost everyone got lost in these new environs. In trying to cope and keep life going for everyone, the young and the able-bodied lost the zest of their youth and the fulcrum of their identities. They could not reconcile with the new reality of rootlessness. Many fell into an abyss of depression. The new generation of Kashmiris that were born in this exile grew up without ever knowing their homeland.

The year was 1993, and our first days of exile in Delhi. Everything changed, and for a time, it seemed only for the worst. The air was filled with soot and grime that would settle on my clothes and in my rather fragile lungs. Some reckoned that the soot and smoke from the congested rush-hour traffic in Delhi those days was among the worst in the world. The air was always filled with dust. I learnt it the hard way when, in a matter of months of commuting to work in the city buses, my lungs came close to packing up. I learnt early from the doctor that I was not to leave the house without my prescription medicine, the two pulmonary pumps of Asthalin and Seriflo. When eye-popping coughing gave way to wheezing, out would come my life-saving pumps. As I took two deep drags of each I could feel the lungs soothe and salve, giving me temporary reprieve from fatigue and breathlessness. This was a new, and wholly unwholesome, experience of life in a metropolitan city whose ground reality is far more sinister than its spit-and-polish image of jobs and plenty that still continue to beckon and tantalize millions of small-town youth every year.

I remember sitting in the 'chartered' buses of Delhi and being filled with dejection and disappointment every day at the sight of the hoary, dull sky that was such a far cry from how it was in the home that I had lost. The faces that I greeted in the bus would manage weary, wan smiles and would soon conceivably be lost in the thoughts of the next battle for survival that lay ahead of them.

I had never reconciled to and recovered from the premature death of my father. That, along with the migration from Kashmir and the daily battles to keep self and family together, dealt deep blows to my emotional health and quietly chipped away at my natural, resilient disposition, leaving me fragile and never too far from a psychological breakdown.

By and by, for the majority that chose to fight back, the need to survive metamorphosed the peace-loving Pandit into a razor sharp, too-clever-by-half, man-about-town of a metropolitan city, a barely recognizable shadow of his former self. In these 28 years, while most in my community have moved out of migrant camps into shelters they can call their own, no one seems to be living in their home. The yearning for going home is there in every heart. As for me, I remain heartbroken that I can no longer see birds flying home in the evenings. But maybe, this is not a ritual among the birds of lands other than Kashmir. Maybe, like me, these city birds are homeless too.

When Slow Death Followed
Murder Most Foul

I was newly arrived in Jammu, leaving behind my home and medical practice due to the militancy in Kashmir. Soon after, patients started flooding the residential clinic that I had rented at New Plots. The variety of clinical presentations was mind-boggling. Back home, I had established myself as an internist and neurologist, but it was different in exile. Displaced people from Kashmir were housed in refugee camps in the desolate suburbs of the city where they lived a cramped existence in tents, bereft of basic amenities, exposed to the vagaries of the harsh climate, and prone to myriad afflictions of body and mind. They had nowhere to go to for a medical consultation except to doctors amongst fellow refugees. They did not care about your speciality; they sought you because you were a Kashmiri physician and because they knew no one else in the alien climes. More importantly, they trusted you for what you had been in Kashmir. It was that trust you were called upon to uphold now. Overwhelmed with patients exhibiting the full gamut of psychiatric syndromes, physical afflictions, and ailments brought forth by life in an unwholesome environment, and other medical conditions hardly observed before in these people, I had to catch up with the knowledge of the numerous disciplines that I had left behind after moving to my sub-speciality.

There could be no compartmentalization in medicine in the changed circumstances of tragic displacement and the terrible consequences thereof.

* * *

It was in this setting that I was called upon in March 1991 to visit a patient who had been unresponsive for 10 days. Suresh was 16, the youngest in a family of five. They had been driven out of the comfort of their pastoral life in Shopian, a town that brought to mind visions of the famous Aharbal Falls, the lush green meadows of Kongwattan, and the high-altitude spring of Kausar Nag, also called Vishnu Paad because legend has it that Lord Vishnu had set his foot on the mountains and created the beautiful foot-shaped spring. The family owned a house and farmland that brought substantial income to sustain them with dignity.

A fortnight earlier, Suresh's elder brother had been abducted by militants. The following day, his body was found in a ditch, staked with a note that warned of dire consequences if anyone dared to remove the corpse from where it had been abandoned. Notwithstanding, his father, Shivji, retrieved the battered body and arranged a hurried, hush-hush funeral ceremony. When his brother was laid on the pyre and the first flames shot up, Suresh suddenly gave a long and agonizing squeal like one possessed, ran to his home and into his room, where he shut himself in. No amount of persuasion would move him to open the door. Fearing the worst, Shivji broke into the room to find him lying in his bed, staring at the ceiling, unresponsive to queries, inert to his ministrations.

Having flouted the warning of the killers, Shivji's life, as well as that of his family members, was in danger. They had nowhere to go to for help since all the administrative institutions in the Valley had collapsed and most of the Pandit neighbours had already fled the horrors of militancy. The only way out was to pack their bare essentials and leave the accursed place as quickly as possible.

The ashes of his murdered son were still warm when Shivji gathered them the next morning from the cremation ground. He hired a taxi and, with the help of the driver, he carried his shell-shocked son into the back seat, resting his head in the lap of his mother, while he sat with his daughter in the front. Arriving in Jammu late in the evening, they sought shelter in a dharamshala.

All through the journey, Suresh remained withdrawn, mute, and unconcerned about what was going on. His eyes were open, but vacant. People around him did not exist. He passively accepted small amounts of fluids including milk, water, and tea, but made no effort to eat, speak, or move. It was a reflex act of swallowing with no voluntary participation. Solid food thrust in his mouth stayed there with no attempt to chew or swallow.

Jammu was an alien town for them; they had no idea where to go and who to consult for Suresh's treatment. The temple priest requested a doctor to make a house call. He prescribed pills that were to be administered after being crushed and dissolved in water. Three days later, finding the patient still unresponsive and unable to swallow properly, he referred him to a psychiatric hospital, which overflowed with patients. Suresh had to share a bed with another patient. He was put on intravenous fluids and medication. His mother and sister took turns to stay by his side while Shivji did the running about. They were distraught from loss of sleep and fatigue, with hardly any help from any quarter and little to eat. On the fourth day at the hospital, Suresh became agitated, struggled to get out of the bed, and pulled out the intravenous line. The doctors restrained him and administered tranquillizers.

Suresh became more somnolent and was unable to swallow even small sips of liquids after that incident. It drove the family to despair and Shivji decided to pull him out of the hospital. That is when the family beseeched me to see him. I was pressed for time from the swarms of patients waiting in the lawn and spilling over on to the street, but sensing their desperation, I agreed to visit the patient.

Suresh was lying on a thin mattress on the floor, a young girl by his side looking mournful and helpless. He had been starving himself, refusing all food and drink. He had not passed any urine for 24 hours. Unwashed and smelling, he lay curled up on his side, legs drawn up flexed at the knees, thighs touching the abdomen, arms folded across the chest, head bent forward, and his chin almost digging into the upper chest. It was the quintessential foetal position, as if he had repositioned himself in his mother's womb, trying to protect himself—from the outside world, from himself.

Examining him was not easy. He didn't respond to any verbal commands except with a barely audible grunt. He was rigid in body and limbs. There was no way to overcome the stiffness and open his arms or legs; when I tried, a hoarse groan escaped his lips. On turning him supine, his torso, with the limbs crossed in front, moved as one block; his eyes screwed shut, his brows knitted, his face contorted. He was wasted, his orbs deep, his lips cracked, a struggling beard on his sunken cheeks, his hair coarse and unkempt. The temperature was sub-normal, the pulse feeble, and the breathing slow and shallow. His abdomen was sunk like a boat as if the viscera had been scooped out such that I could palpate the vertebrae under the abdominal wall. His heart beat feebly, his bladder felt empty.

It was a picture of total retreat from the outside world, as if he were hiding within himself. I was reminded of the practice of Santhara prevalent in the Jain ascetics who decide to quit the earth and starve themselves to death.

It was evident that severe depression as a result of catastrophic stress from the gruesome murder of his brother and the terrifying spectacle of his body burning on the pyre had precipitated the clinical syndrome. Managing such a serious patient was neither easy nor possible at home. He might need electroconvulsive therapy—a procedure in which electric current is passed through the brain.

My suggestion to the parents to get him re-admitted fell flat. 'We are literally on the road with nobody to fall back upon. We have tried the hospital but came out worse from there. Please, let him be here; we will do as you bid us. If you could only make him eat and drink, he might recover by and by,' his father pleaded.

'We will need to rehydrate him with intravenous infusions. Until he starts eating on his own he will need to be fed through a tube in the stomach. His bladder has to be catheterized to let the urine flow freely without soiling the bed. He needs physiotherapy so he does not develop bedsores and contractures. All that cannot be done here in this temple,'

I explained. But it did not quite sink in. 'If you introduce the catheter and the stomach tube and teach us how to go about feeding him, we will run a 24-hour vigil on him, and follow your instructions in letter and spirit. But we beg of you, please do not send him to the mental hospital again. He is not out of his senses, not mad. He was fine before the tragedy struck us. He has been a bright student, always among the top in his class. He was preparing hard for his matriculation examination and we had great expectations from him.'

The boy's parents looked at me imploringly, their hands folded in supplication, the mother weeping torrentially. 'The hospital is a bedlam; my son will die there!' she wailed.

I waited until Shivji came back from the pharmacy with a feeding tube, catheter, aspirating syringe, and the medicines that I prescribed. We lifted the boy from the floor and placed him on a string-cot loaned by the priest. I introduced the in-dwelling catheter into the bladder, attached the free end to the urine sac, and let the bag hang from the bed.

Next I pushed the feeding tube through one nostril and advanced it down the food pipe into the stomach. We pushed water slowly with the syringe into the feeding tube.

I directed them to feed the patient small and frequent—just about 100–150 ml—aliquots of fruit juice, milk, soup, and water every hour during the day, and to administer the medicines regularly. They could rest during the night.

I reiterated my instructions: 'Before every feed, you must aspirate some fluid from the stomach to make sure that the tube is in place. Keep your eyes and ears open; if he coughs or chokes while you are feeding him, it could be an indication that the tube has got displaced. In that case, you should stop, otherwise food can go into the air passages. That will be disastrous.'

I asked them to report progress every day and drove off, not without some misgivings even as they were overwhelmed and thanked me profusely.

The feeding went on for a few days without any complications and the urine flowed freely, more than a litre a day. But the boy made no improvement on other fronts. He continued to remain withdrawn, mute, and huddled up, and repulsed any attempts at physiotherapy. On the fifth day, they reported fever, chills, and mild cough. Did they ensure the feeding tube was in the stomach? I asked. They were sure it was. Was the urine flowing freely? Yes, it was.

I prescribed antibiotics, suspecting either urinary tract infection or hypostatic pneumonia, but the fever did not respond over the next three days and Suresh's mental and physical state remained unchanged. They pressed me to visit him a second time, but my schedule was so tight I hardly got time to eat or rest during that first year of exile. I insisted that they take him to the hospital and wrote a referral letter.

Two days later, as I was winding up my morning clinic that had stretched into the afternoon, a patient was brought in an unconscious state, accompanied by a frenzied crowd in which I spotted Suresh's parents.

'Doctor Sahib, please save her. Or give us poison before we are left childless,' cried Shivji, while the mother sat by the side of the patient, screaming, beating her chest. I was shocked to find them devastated.

'Who is she?' I asked.

'She is our daughter, Vandhana. You saw her the other day when you visited us in the temple.'

I looked at the girl on the examining couch. Her eyes were shut; she was crouched like her brother, immobile and unresponsive.

'How long has she been like this?'

'Since yesterday... Doctor Sahib, please do something, she is all that is left of our children now.'

'What!'

'Suresh died yesterday. I have yet to gather his ashes. Those of his brother still wait to be immersed in the Ganges. Now it seems it is our daughter's turn! She went into this state when she watched her brother in his death throes.'

'What happened to him?'

'After we left your clinic the last time we met you, we called in another doctor instead of taking Suresh to the hospital as you had advised. He prescribed a different set of drugs. But the next day, Suresh started coughing at every feed. We called in a chemist who runs a shop in the village nearby. He surmised that the feeding tube was only half way down the food pipe.

He pushed it further down and fed him milk through the syringe, but Suresh coughed and resisted. The chemist asked us to restrain him while he tried to push more milk through the tube. Suresh coughed harder, choked, and turned blue. He stopped breathing and convulsed and fell limp on the bed. It all happened so suddenly.'

It was heart-wrenching, but I had no time to shed tears for this young boy or to empathize with his parents for the cruel death of both their sons within a fortnight. Now their only surviving offspring lay crouched on the couch, in desperate need of my full attention.

* * *

This tragic turn of events in the family was emblematic of the terrible times we were passing through. No doubt, those were the early dark days of our violent displacement from Kashmir, full of tragic events beyond our control, during which we lost thousands of lives, many more than were done to death by the militants in Kashmir. But that was poor consolation for the loss of yet another precious life that should have been saved.

— As told by Dr Kundan Lal Chowdhury

On the Run, I Filled Up My Empty Spaces Again

Thirty years ago, I had enrolled on a Masters degree at a communications school with borderline pedagogical tradition and not much pressure on students to perform. It didn't take me long to notice Rabia's unique creative energy and her natural gift for nonchalance. We made friends in no time. Her displacement journey criss-crossed with mine. We stayed in and out of touch as our paths diverged. For years, Rabia has been busy shaping new creative buds at a premier communications school in Mumbai, India. Through multiple extreme trials that have tested her mettle, she remains her ethereal self, a woman of substance blithely going about her life as a child of destiny. To me, she defines beauty, wit, and strength packed into one fragile body that could give way at any time.

From a very young age, when I was around three, I recollect a sense of fear and uselessness that overwhelmed me all the time. My grandmother, who I was given to, had become like a sanctuary that I never wanted to step out of. I used to cling on to her like a baby kangaroo. Even the separation for a few hours of school was not a good feeling, and on returning home I would run back to her as if I had found her all over again. At that age I did not have the understanding or the capacity to question this feeling but I was very clear about a few things even at that age. For example, I would not look into a mirror very often. There were two reasons: one, I was not able to face the fact that I am not good-looking. The second reason was my eyes—I didn't want to look into them because of the frightening questions and the desperation to break free that I saw there.

I had a lot questions in my mind. I was labelled a rebel. I was not. I was a liberal without the jargon to justify it. Very early in life, I realized that if a woman is a liberal, she is automatically pronounced a rebel.

I was born into an upper-middle-class, highly educated, and very well-known family of Kashmir. I was four months old when I was given away to my grandmother, Zainab, because my mother had already become pregnant with my little sister. They said she was too young to take care of two children almost the same age. But she was old enough to bake a hundred rotis, endless pots of food and *samovars* of tea. The labour-intensive chores of a Kashmiri household were always lighter than the matters of heart and mind. Women were expected to stick to the former.

I was loved and nurtured by my grandmother like a prized possession. I aped everything she did. She was my hero, and my world—a warm, well-kept, and an adventurous world. I grew up into a strong, independent, stubborn, and a little broken girl. Listening to stories of compassion, swimming endlessly in the dew-like waters of Botakadal, trekking up the hills of Shankaracharya, growing organic vegetables in the backyard, and naming hens and roosters after popular film stars was what my childhood was made of. I loved sports and eventually wanted to join the army. Physical fitness and the lives of the armed forces fascinated me no end. This passion for sports led me to explore the city of Kashmir more then my peers. I formed a very personal and intimate connection with the mountains, valleys, and streams of my home town. It was more or less a very peculiar love story between my space and me.

My world turned upside down when my parents decided to take me back to the family that I had never belonged to. I was suddenly pushed out of my world into a space that was cold, hostile, and lonely. With this one move, my childhood turned to a living hell. My existence was more like a broken limb, limping lifelessly in pain and agony. I broke like a sheet of glass into tiny pieces that I still cannot fix fully. The bunch of strangers who claimed to be my own never acknowledged the trauma I was going through. When I overcame the initial numbness, I determinedly and helplessly tried to escape. Every day I would run away from school and hold on to my grandmother till I was dragged back again to my parents' house in the evening. My grandmother and I fought, cried, protested, and pleaded, but the members of my highly educated family had turned into unfeeling, indifferent strangers. I kept sobbing for months in the lonely nights of 47 Kathi Darwaza, Rainawari, and my grandmother kept weeping in the moonlit balconies of Madin Sahib Hawal. This distance of 5 km between the two houses was the longest ever. One day, the inevitable happened.

I was rushed to the hospital with alarmingly high blood sugar levels. Diagnosed with stress-induced juvenile diabetes, I spent months in the hospital and everyone around seemed shattered. The realization of the sin committed hit the family hard, but it was too late. The life of an 11-year-old sports freak had turned into a portable pharmacy. Insulin injections and blood tests is what I was reduced to. It hurt everyone around me, but then cause does become a curse at times.

My new role as a teenager was quite vague. No deliverables, no standards, no scores, literally nothing was expected of me. I was left alone to do whatever I wished. The agenda was now further complicating the already complicated state of heath I was in. This new role, though, pushed me a bit closer to exploring the world of the Nazkis, and unexpectedly, I started liking it too. My paternal grandfather became my self-proclaimed anchor. I looked up to him and drew immense strength from the man and discarded him the moment it didn't suit me. I still could not demolish the wall between my parents and me but my two younger siblings became the phoenix of my new life. They healed me to a large extent.

Vishwabharti College for Women gave me a new identity. I started looking into the mirror with no fear. I looked into my eyes and faced all my demons. And I decided to take them head on. A new me emerged. Dreams, desires, aspirations, and expectations started sprouting within me. A sense of direction and a focus evolved. Things or ideologies that were thrust on me were thrown back with the same intensity. By the end of my graduation, at just 18 years old, I broke the engagement with my first cousin that I had never given consent to. All hell broke loose but it was important to create my own heaven.

After completing my graduation, I joined the department of mass communication at Kashmir University. I fell in love with the campus at first sight. I felt vibrant, free, and alive after so many years. And it surely left an impact on others. For the first time in my life, I made friends: Kumar, Parvaiz, Muslim, Aliya, Nasir, Izhar, and Nawaz. I found a set of people with different personalities but a common compassion. We lived separately but dreamt together. The intense relationship with this bunch replaced the drought within me into a lushness that brought forth much-needed peace and harmony. This was the roller-coaster part of my life, as I went through so many different emotions, discovered vulnerabilities, and found love. I was happy and how—but that was not going to last for too long.

In 1989, we were in the last year of our postgraduate education, ready to fly, but fate had different plans. On 8 December 1989, a Kashmiri Muslim militant organization kidnapped Rubaiya Sayeed, the daughter of Mufti Mohammad Sayeed, the then home minister of India, and demanded the release of five of their militants in exchange for her release. I was shocked. I heard the word militant for the first time in the context of Kashmir. More than being concerned about the advent of militancy in my home state, I was morally disturbed about the fact that our youth disrespected the sanctity of a woman. I was too naïve to understand the magnitude of the problem that would uproot the ethos and culture of a place that fed on Rishism and Sufism. In no time, in the very same place, 'gun' became intrinsic to its culture and blood painted us red.

The exodus of the Kashmiri Pandits came in their life as the worst nightmare. For me and many Muslims like me, it planted a huge sense of guilt and shame within us. The helplessness of not being able to protect them still haunts me. When my Pandit brethren lost their home that day, I too lost the feeling of home.

My father was the director of Radio Kashmir, the hugely popular radio station that is part of the federal state-owned radio network of India, when the armed conflict was at its peak. An Indian by conviction, he knew things were going to be difficult. It was not an easy stand to take at that point of time. And all of us had to pay for it heavily. Our family was on the hit list of every militant organization. Many relatives, friends, and well-wishers advised my father to either leave his job or just take a transfer to a safer place. He didn't. Every moment, we would spend anticipating an attack on my father and die a hundred deaths. Threats, unsuccessful attacks, and attempted kidnappings became a part of our life. With this deathly sound of Kalashnikovs and a full-fledged insurgency, we lived in a battlefield.

The entire population was out on the street of Srinagar, shouting azadi slogans. On the fateful night of 13 February 1990, I answered two phone calls. The first one that came on the landline was of Uncle Lasa Kaul, director, Doordarshan Kendra Srinagar, the provincial arm of the national television broadcaster of India. He was a very close friend of my father. I told him to hold on till I woke my father up. He asked me not to as he would speak to him in office the day after. We chatted a bit and he asked me what we had cooked for dinner. He was missing homemade food that he had not eaten for a long time. Due to repeated threats from militant groups, he lived in heavily guarded government accommodation. His wife and two children had migrated to Delhi but his parents had decided to stay back in Srinagar till he was there. The second phone call that came sends shivers down my spine even now. The most painful and frightening turn of events. Militants had killed Lassa Kaul, outside his house in Bemina, when he had sneaked out to see his old parents. The next target was my father, they said.

We were asked to shift to a safer place immediately, especially my father. After some time, heavily guarded police vehicles came and took him to a secret destination. Early next morning, my brother, sister, mother, and I were flown to Delhi. For months together we did not see our father. He was in Srinagar and we were in Delhi. Lost and uprooted, hurt and scared, we were living a nightmare. We knew things were never going be the same. We lived in a constant state of threat, insecurity, and fear. At 21, my dreams were shattered yet again.

After spending some months in Delhi, my mother went back to Kashmir to be with my father. My brother was sent to study medicine in Hyderabad and my sister stated working in Jammu. I took up a research assistant's job in MCRC Jamia. After a lot of difficulty, I managed to get a room in the working girls' hostel at Jamia Millia Islamia, Delhi.

An independent life free of parental control was ahead of me, but I had lost the capacity to welcome it. An overwhelming sense of emptiness and loneliness had engulfed me. The normal desires or aspirations of a 22-year-old had taken a back seat. My parents did their best to shield us from the horrors of the conflict back home, but the gore was impossible to conceal. From the safety of the hostel, I would keep imagining the familiar hell that I had left behind. Stories of people being forced from their homes and the bloodshed were all that filled my mind. With every death in the Valley, something died within me.

Before long, hundreds of Kashmiri students, trying to escape the uncertainty in Kashmir, came flocking to Jamia Millia for their college admission. Everybody seemed to be on the run. Some acknowledged it and some just preferred to deny the crisis. Initially, people in Delhi were sympathetic, but slowly a subtle resistance towards the Kashmiris surfaced. It was the same resistance that the Kashmiri Pandits faced in Jammu. Here too, the locals felt that we were binging on their resources and they didn't like it. I so vividly remember an incident that took place in our hostel. A girl in the hostel screamed and yelled at me for occupying the room that she deserved. She humiliated and insulted me, calling me a refugee. Of all the wounds of unsettlement, being called a refugee was the most difficult one to soothe. In your own country, words like refugee or migrant created an unsettling feeling that stayed for a long time. I was slowly losing my grit and the only response left was to cry, not for me but for Kashmir.

In 1992, I got married to my best friend, Parvaiz. We were happy, trying to find a home, fighting challenges, re-assembling an identity, creating a sense of community, and making new memories. Despite a growing hostile attitude towards Kashmiri Muslims, we were busy rebuilding ourselves anew, brick by brick. But the feeling of being in exile always held me hostage. We kept receiving news of lost or killed friends and relatives, and the fear of losing my father to militancy didn't leave me for a minute. My pleasant memories from the past started hurting me more than the ones that were unpleasant. I pined for the Kashmir that I grew up in and constantly worried about my parents who were all alone in the Valley.

Pregnancy after a month of my marriage came as a breath of fresh air. I was on cloud nine, but the nightmares of loss of peace, the death of my dear friend Nasir, and the deadly armed attack on my uncle were at the back of my mind. My pregnancy was chaotic and my health went for a toss. I was advised to terminate the pregnancy, which I did not want to do at any cost. Initially, Parvaiz too wanted me to get the procedure done, but when I refused, he stood like a rock behind me. We were the same age, but he nursed me like a mother. He wouldn't leave me alone for a moment and saw to it that our financial crisis did not bother me much. In the seventh month of my pregnancy, an ultrasound revealed that everything was fine with the baby. Both of us were relieved by these reports and started planning for the baby eagerly. I was happy, but there was an ominous feeling that was running simultaneously in mind. And it was not in vain. One day, after coming back from my morning walk, my neighbour called out and showed me the morning paper. The headline said that the militants had kidnapped my two uncles and cousin and had demanded the release of three militants in exchange. I started shaking and fell down. Parvaiz came running and screamed at the neighbour. He already knew about this but didn't want me to know. I went through hell till I got the news of their release 15 days later. The next evening we celebrated their release, only to step into an agony-filled phase of our life.

My blood pressure shot up all of a sudden and I started bleeding. The doctors decided to take the baby out. A highly qualified doctor was called in to take care of the baby when my operation started. We kept waiting for the paediatrician that we had called for but she didn't turn up for a long time and, in an emergency, they started the procedure. I was in a bad condition and nobody paid attention to my child. After delivering him, the doctors and nurses all thought he was dead, and put him in a bin. After they stitched me up and I stabilized a bit, I asked for my child. They kept ignoring my request. When I started screaming and yelling at them, one of the junior doctors snapped at me saying that my child was dead. Tears rolling down my cheeks, I insisted on seeing him. They picked him up from the bin to show him to me and my baby started moving his hand. Suddenly, all of them realized that he was alive. I was overjoyed. I held him for a while and then they took him away. They handed the baby to my parents when he should have been rushed to an incubator, as he was a premature child. Suddenly, my father realized that the baby was turning blue. He rushed him to the doctor and he was put in an incubator. For a good two hours he was not given oxygen. After a year, we came to know that the lack of oxygen supply to the brain at that time had led to cerebral palsy in my child. My son never walked.

When you are going through a difficult time, having a family around dilutes the pain. My parents did try their best to support us during the most difficult phase of our lives, but the physical distance between Kashmir and

Delhi was becoming a barrier. No doubt they would come running to us as and when we needed, but it didn't feel right to keep calling them all the time. Both Parvaiz and I were devastated by the state our son, Qismat, was in. Struggling to come to terms with his disability, we desperately needed someone to hold us together. It was the first time in our relationship of five years that we were not able to console, and find solace in, each other. Both of us were too emotionally broken to be of any comfort to each other. I was becoming obsessive about Qismat, and Parvaiz was retreating deeper into a shell. For me, it was a war that I needed to win. For him, it must have been an equal hell. The truth was that it was incredibly tough to get used to having a child with special needs. On top of everything, the most draining part was to suffer the prejudices and insensitivities of others. You don't get much more vulnerable than by having children with special needs.

No child with special needs is responsible for a marriage dissolving, but the difficult circumstances did take a toll on us. One day, I walked out of the marriage. We separated when Qismat was just eight years old. I take a lot of pride in bringing up Qismat the way I did, but I stand guilty for not being able to hold together a family that he so needed.

I shifted to Mumbai in 2002 with a broken marriage, a son whom I had to leave behind, massive psychological issues, and a few unfulfilled dreams. Everything and anything that I thought was mine ceased to be so. The only person who stood like a rock behind me was my sister Roohi— non-judgemental, fair and honest. The first thing that she did was to take me to a counsellor and get some semblance of normalcy in my distraught life. Now that I look back, I feel that had this intervention come earlier, I may have been able to salvage a lot more in my life. I had left everything behind—a husband, a house, financial security, and a child I loved madly. No doubt I was lost and confused; yet, I felt I was close to what I seemed to have been searching for. Rediscovering myself, I stepped out of my comfort zone, took unbelievable risks, recovered some confidence, and embarked on a journey that I had left incomplete.

Mumbai was a game-changer of sorts. The sense of belonging that I felt in this place was surprising. In many ways I was similar to these people, and in many ways, different, yet they never seemed to make me feel alien in this land of theirs. Everyone had wonderful stories to tell and I loved listening to them. Here, in this city, I realized the meaning of accepting other people's differences. Acceptance did not mean agreement, and debate was not at all a disagreement. Mumbai became the place that took Kashmir away from me. It cleared out a lot of space that I could fill up with much more.

Mumbai became home—a home that I had missed for years. It became a temperament that I had yearned to be accepted for. It became a spirit that I loved. It became everything that made me acceptable and valuable. No doubt it threw challenges at me, but it also gave me the strength to conquer them. It kept me on my toes, but gave me the wings to fly. For the last 15 years, I have been in Mumbai, but Kashmir stays in my heart for ever. The Kashmir I miss and long for is not the Kashmir I go to every year. It is the Kashmir that I grew up in. For me, Kashmir is not a breathtakingly beautiful piece of landscape. It is the personification of tranquillity and peace, which it hasn't been for a long time. When I visit Kashmir, the mountains are full of gloom, the streams and rivers are screaming in pain, the gardens are lonely, and the chinars are sad. I cannot bear this sight and I run back to where I belong. Mumbai hugs me tight and I go off to sleep, holding Kashmir in my arms all night.

IRAQ

'The free world cannot afford to accept any form of extremism, whether it is fascism, racism or religious extremism.'

Widad Akreyi

A country in Western Asia, Iraq is bordered by Turkey to the north, Iran to the east, Kuwait to the southeast, Saudi Arabia to the south, Jordan to the southwest, and Syria to the west.

As of 2016, Iraq had a population of more than 37 million. The total number of IDPs by reason of conflict and violence exceeded 3 million, with new displacements in the same category during 2016 being 659,000.

Historically, displacement in Iraq has been driven by a combination of internal armed conflict, generalized violence, and persecution on the basis of political affiliation, ethnicity, or religious background.

I Hear the Yezidis Have Been Hounded Out Before

Getting into war zones is not easy if you are not an accredited media person or an aid worker cleared by the host government. Suspicions about foreigners run high. Access is denied for the flimsiest of reasons that are often not explained. Reaching the Yezidi camps in the semi-autonomous Kurdistan region of northern Iraq was an act of serendipity, pure and simple. So, first, the backstory: In August of 2015, all attempts to secure a visa from the Kurdistan Regional Government had come to nothing. Since I was travelling in the region, I decided to take a chance with the Kurdish immigration authorities. I hopped onto a plane from Izmir in Turkey and reached Erbil via Istanbul. Failing to produce the visa at the Passport Control in Erbil, I was promptly accompanied to the chief immigration officer at Erbil International Airport. The officer, without any fuss whatsoever, treating me as a serious offender, impounded my passport and let me spend the next 20 hours on an iron bench outside his office. When it was time for the return flight to Istanbul, a junior intelligence officer surfaced out of nowhere, held me by the hand, and walked me to the Turkish Airlines counter to have my ticket to my home country processed. My deportation formalities completed, the passport was delivered in a sealed envelope to the head flight purser who was instructed to let me board the plane after all passengers had boarded and be allotted a seat in the tail end of the plane. Upon reaching our destination, she was advised to personally hand me over to the Turkish immigration authorities in Istanbul. In Istanbul, I received my passport, the ticket, and the boarding card for my onward journey to Delhi.

Clearly, I had grossly underestimated the risks of travelling without a visa to war zones and overestimated my ability to hoodwink hard-nosed, young, and dashing Kurdish immigration sleuths into handing me the keys to their region simply because I looked earnest and, as a former aid worker-turned-writer/researcher, meant well.

By sheer happenstance, less than six months later, I had the opportunity to travel—on a legitimate work permit—to Dohuk, one of the three governorates that comprise the Kurdistan region of Iraq. On this occasion,

I was on an assignment with the World Health Organization (WHO) as part of a five-member international evaluation team tasked with reviewing the National Tuberculosis Control Programme in Iraq. It was during this mission that I visited the Yezidi camps in Dohuk and met with Anis and Khidir. A Kurdish colleague accompanying the mission facilitated the difficult conversation as I sat down to listen to the searing account of radical terror that swept through the Yezidi community in the days when Daesh stormed through their villages. The telltale accounts of sudden dispossession and unspeakable crimes committed against the young and defenceless Yezidi girls and women surpassed the stories that I had hitherto been aware of from other parts of the world.

Habo, my son, is just 16. Daesh took him. Sadiq, my brother, is also the same age as Habo. They took him too. When the Daesh came to Til Qasab, our village, they were home together with my 20-year-old cousin, Husain, and one of my brothers-in-law. They took all of them. It has been more than a year and we know nothing about their whereabouts.

A day came when we knew it was time to leave our homes and run for safety. Daesh was closing in on us, having taken our neighbouring villages. Desperate and fearful friends and relatives who were encircled by Daesh called frantically, asking us to run for safety before it was too late. The whole village of some 15,000 houses emptied out in no time. The elderly, women, men, and children, we all headed for the Sinjar Mountains. Word had come that the terrorists were camping in the valley and the mountains would be beyond their reach as no one lived there. As we were leaving, many of the young men were filled with a rush of blood at having to leave their homes and show their backs to the terrorists. They decided to stay back and fight for their homeland. The male members of my family, who we have now lost without a trace, were also among those youth. We learnt that the boys were taken by Daesh near the main checkpoint at Sinjar.

Two of my maternal uncles are also missing. One of them was 50 and the head of a family of 20 members. All his children were married and living under the same roof. Another uncle too had almost the same number of family members. They took their time coming to a decision about whether to stay back or follow others to the safety of the mountain, and by then the entire family was taken by Daesh, including their women. All of them.

From this family, we have had one of the daughters-in-law returned to us. They found her in Raqqa in Syria. We learnt that Daesh was selling her for USD 10,000, which my mother's cousins and others in the extended family somehow managed to collect and pay for her release. Just like her, thousands of our Yezidi women have been taken by Daesh as objects of trade and their honour violated by being subjected to unspeakable atrocities. Another woman we managed to get back is a cousin of mine. The deal took place in Mosul where a Daesh captor had put a price of USD 10,600 on her release.

Til Qasab is no small hamlet in Sinjar; it is a rather large town. I can tell you that each and every person or family who stayed back—perhaps no more than 10 per cent of all inhabitants—is now in the custody of Daesh. The village is a no-go area for the Peshmerga, our Kurdish fighting forces. The town is in a valley, and access from the Syrian border is not difficult. It was among the first Yezidi towns that Daesh occupied.

None of our non-Yezidi Arab neighbours came to our rescue. The Yezidis who got killed in the process of running for cover to the Sinjar Mountains were, in fact, blocked by the Arabs from reaching there. It is clear to us that our neighbours from another religion were not interested in saving our lives. These were neighbours that we had lived with for hundreds of years. I hate to think about those days. I don't want to relive those painful memories. But I saw everything. I was there. It felt like the world was out to annihilate the entire Yezidi community. Never before in history have we been killed in such large numbers. Indeed, there would be few parallels in history to the sufferings of the Yezidis. Yezidi suffering, if history is to be believed, dates back thousands of years, but we have, and will continue to persevere, and survive. And we will go on.

I have traumatic memories of seeing the Daesh fighters roaming our streets with their guns. They would come in large groups to our homes, search the house, and take away young men and women. They took Zidan, my husband, thrice, and each time he managed to run away. He is a Peshmerga soldier. It must be his training as a soldier that saved him. But my son and other family members were not so lucky.

These terrorists looked nothing like the local people from Sinjar, but since I have not seen people from other parts of Iraq, I cannot say if they were Iraqis or others.

Can you please help the Yezidi people? We have suffered a lot. So many of our young people have been killed or kidnapped. Others are risking dangerous journeys by boats to migrate to other countries. There is pain in every mother's heart. If you could get back Sinjar for us from these monsters, we would simply go back to our land. We do not want anything more.

For the time that we are condemned to live in this camp, I just want us to be treated like human beings. Yezidi women have very low expectations from life. I never went to school. I was hardly an adult when I was married. I am a mother to six children and looking after them is all that I do. Here in the camp, I think all the time about our women, men, and our lands that have been snatched away. How can we survive without our youth or our lands? We just want to go home.

* * *

A UN report issued on 2 October 2014, based on 500 interviews with witnesses, said that ISIS took 450–500 women and girls to Iraq's Nineveh region in August where '150 unmarried girls and women, predominantly from the Yazidi and Christian communities, were reportedly transported to Syria, either to be given to ISIL fighters as a reward or to be sold as sex slaves'. Also in October 2014, a UN report revealed that ISIL had detained 5,000–7,000 Yezidi women as slaves or forced brides in north Iraq in August 2014.

In 2014, over 5,000 members of the Yezidi community are estimated to have been killed at the hands of Daesh. Thousands of their women were abducted and sold into sex slavery. The mass killings and abductions of the Yezidis led to their expulsion, flight, and effectively, exile from their ancestral lands in north Iraq, where the Yezidi community largely lived, in the Nineveh province. Some half a million Yezidis now live as refugees in their own land.

Living in a Camp Is Never Easy

When ISIS (another name for Daesh) first occupied the villages of Girzirk and Shiba Sheikh Khidir close to my village, Girzha, our phones did not stop ringing. There was only one message. The Peshmerga were no longer able to stop the advance of ISIS. There was deathly fear in the voices of people trapped in those villages. It was clear that Daesh would be at our doorstep within days. We had to escape. There was only one place thought safe from the Daesh footprint—the barren and quite uninhabitable plateau on top of the Sinjar Mountains, a good 10-km trek away.

My mother, an ailing old lady who was with us on this journey, somehow made it to the mountaintop. Many others that we had seen along the way were not so lucky. At least 10 members of my extended family died on the way. We travelled in our vehicle upto a point on the pass that was motorable and beyond which vehicles couldn't go. So we simply got out and started walking. Others were doing the same to make it out of the village as quickly as possible.

Along the way, we saw a small corridor, which is a point of passage between the Kurdistan region and Syria. There is a bridge on a river that you cross to reach the Syrian side. On and off, when the Peshmerga were in control of security, this corridor would be open for Kurdish people to cross into Syria. On other days when the threat of Daesh was close, the point would be closed. When we got close to the point, we saw that the passage was open and people were frantically crossing over to the other side. We too walked as fast as our legs allowed us, until we reached the town of Derik on the Syrian side.

We stayed there for a few days, but decided to get back into Iraqi Kurdistan at the first opportunity. As we crossed back into our country, we found the Kurdish people to be warm and welcoming. We went to occupy almost any space that provided us a semblance of shelter: school compounds, unfinished buildings, parks, and even spaces under the bridges. In a matter of months, proper camps came to be established.

I have seven boys and two girls. Four of my sons are married and my two daughters will be married soon. A part of my family, including my mother, one son who is married and his children, my two daughters, my wife, and I all live together in two adjacent tents. My other children have been accommodated in another section of the camp, some distance away.

Living in a camp is never easy, but in these days of no income and no work, it entitles us to receive some essential services such as food rations, clothes, and even medicine. We are registered and recorded as internally displaced by the government. It gives us a stake and a legitimacy that we need as we begin to rebuild our lives.

We receive no cash assistance or indeed any discernible form of social protection, something that we desperately need. An NGO has started a kindergarten that admits some of the toddlers from the camp. At this school, some international agencies screen children for chronic illnesses. Those that are found ill are taken to the general hospital in Dohuk and sometimes even to private health facilities for treatment. However, for others, including the elderly, no such facilities exist.

On a couple of occasions, a good samaritan showed up in the camp and distributed medicines among the residents. He is the brother of a woman member of parliament who represents the Yezidi population in the national legislature. The medicines were meant for the treatment of chronic illnesses.

Stress and psychological issues are the most common among children and young people alike. A park or a sports facility at the camp would really help everyone to unwind and serve as a form of psycho-social support.

Food is a big need. The food articles distributed by UN agencies are not edible. Because of joblessness and rapidly dwindling savings, we can hardly afford to buy even essential provisions from the open markets. In these circumstances, distributing quality food articles is critical to survival of the camp residents.

Long power shutdowns are a norm in the camp. It is winter still and these days we get electricity from 6 a.m. to 8 a.m., and then again from 4 p.m. to 11 p.m. If such a scenario continues in the coming summer months, this place is going to turn into a living hell. Just as agencies such as UNICEF distributed winter clothes in the Yezidi camps for all age groups, we need similar assistance to cope with the coming summer months.

The Yezidis are leaving their lands and migrating to Europe in waves. Many are falling prey to human smugglers who charge them massive sums of money to help them travel to Europe and other places, for the most part via Turkey. I know other people, such as the Syrians, Iraqis, and Afghans, are also migrating in the same way. Our situation is stark. We either wither or migrate.

Why can't there be special international agencies looking into our needs? Better still, the international community could provide us with safe havens on the lines of the safe havens that were provided to the Kurds after the uprising in 1991. These safe havens could be located in the plains of Mosul or those liberated areas that are under government control.

MYANMAR

'It's not power that corrupts but fear.'

Aung San Suu Kyi

The Rohingya people are a Muslim minority group residing in Rakhine State, formerly known as Arakan, in Myanmar.

The Rohingya people are considered 'stateless entities', as the Myanmar government has been refusing to recognize them as one of the ethnic groups of the country. For this reason, they lack legal protection from the government, are regarded as mere refugees from Bangladesh, and face strong hostility in the country. They have often been described as one of the most persecuted people on earth.

More than 606,000 people are estimated to have fled from Myanmar to escape attacks on their communities in the western state of Rakhine. Of these, more than 400,000 have escaped since late August 2017 alone.

Then a Storm Began to Brew

My name is Noor Kadir. I am 27 years old. I am a Muslim belonging to the Rohingya community and our home is in the state of Rakhine in western Myanmar. For almost two years, I have been living in Kolkata after being rescued by a shipping company when the boat I was travelling in capsized in the Bay of Bengal.

While still in Rakhine, I married a Muslim man from the same community and we had two children. We were very poor and led a life full of hardship. There was never much money for food or clothing. We could not even buy milk for our children.

This is because my husband did not have a job, and that wasn't because he was lazy or did not want to work. He is a good man and wanted very much to take care of his family. It's just that in Myanmar, Rohingyas are treated like criminals and not allowed to work.

Rohingya Muslims are segregated from the rest of the Rakhine population—the majority Buddhist community—and confined in virtual concentration camps on the fringes of the state. Since my childhood I have lived in such camps designated for our community.

We have never been allowed to go out of these designated areas, not even to the market to buy groceries and other provisions. Curfew was relaxed at the whims of the government which would arbitrarily allow us an hour or so once a week to go out, but only under the watchful eyes of the police and other security personnel. In fact, there used to be permanent police check posts with armed security men situated around the camps so that we could not escape.

We never even had schools built for us. Some learned community elders opened makeshift madrasas and taught the children. Usually, only boys attend, because Muslim girls are married off early and not expected to be too educated. Their parents prefer them to stay at home and master the skills of domestic chores so that they will be useful in their in-laws' homes.

But in our community, even the boys could not attend the classes regularly or for long. Most of them would be sent off by their families to work in Malaysia, Thailand, or Indonesia. Even little children, as young as eight or nine, would be sent off to work. It used to be heartbreaking for their families and they would cry for days afterwards, but there was no other choice, because getting a job in Myanmar was not an option.

We used to hear horror stories about the children, men, and women who had gone off in search of work to these distant places, about being sold off as slaves or forced to work long gruelling hours without food, being beaten and tortured. We even heard rumours that when they fell sick from exhaustion, they would be simply left to die or even killed. However, there was no way to ascertain the truth behind such stories, because none of these reports could be confirmed. Once they left, their families in Rakhine did not hear from them in most cases. Only the lucky few got news of their loved ones.

Some members of the community do have cell phones and are richer than the rest of us. It is they who make it possible for the families to talk to the ones who have gone off to other countries. It is also these same people who bring news of jobs. They travel to distant places and come back with electronic gadgets, garments, and other goods. Since they are part of the community, other members put their trust in them while sending their children off with them to work outside Myanmar. But very often, it is these very people who sell off the children, men, and women by luring them away with promises of lucrative jobs and stories of exciting lives.

While some really want to help, others are just thoroughly bad people. It is hard to tell who is genuine and who is a trafficker. Whatever the case, it is they who make all the arrangements for travel, including organizing a boat or ship. While most families desperate for jobs willingly send off their dear ones, there are those who don't want to. But these people often convince them, saying, 'Why are you afraid? Your child or son or daughter or husband can lead so much of a better life if they get a job in Thailand or Indonesia or Malaysia. They can also send money home. What kind of a life are you leading now? What future does your child have here? Don't you want to change your life for the better? Don't you want them to do well? So many people, young children, men, and women, have gone from here and are earning good money and living a much better life. Don't you see how so-and-so's life has changed for the better since their young son went with me to Malaysia?'

Sometimes, in order to convince reluctant families back in Myanmar, these traffickers arrange for someone living in one of these countries to call home, and then use that as an example of how well he or she is doing. But will any son, daughter, or husband tell their families back home that they are not doing fine? That they are having a hard time or that they are living a hellish life? No, they will not say that. Instead they will say they are fine so that their people don't worry about them. And this is used by these traffickers to lure other people. What people forget is that there are so many others who have never been heard from since their departure. But there is always hope, that maybe things will be fine for their dear one.

In fact, this is why I allowed my husband to go off to Malaysia. Not that he was looking for my approval. We are mere women. Men don't listen to us. When he told me that he had decided to take the offer of a job in Malaysia as a construction helper, I was really reluctant to let him go. I had heard all those horror stories and my instinct told me it was not a good decision. I pleaded with him, 'Don't go, don't go. What will happen to me if anything happens to you? What will happen to our two little children?' He told me, 'What kind of life am I giving you and the children here? Don't you think I feel ashamed as a husband and a father that my wife and children cannot even get two square meals a day? I want to change that. Now I have the opportunity.' I told him that while this life was full of hardship at least we were together. I told him I was happy with whatever little Allah provided for us. I reminded him of all the tales of horror that float in from across the sea.

He chided me and said, 'Don't listen to all those rumours.' He started narrating a list of all the people who have done well for themselves after going off to work in Indonesia, Malaysia, and Thailand.

I eventually decided that there was no point in arguing with him. And it is true that our life was a living hell as it was. Then I started hoping for a better future too. At least for my children.

He was crammed into a boat along with hundreds of other men, women, and children. That was the last time I saw him. But he did call me every so often. Our neighbour had a cell phone and he would ring them up and ask to speak to me. He said he had got a job as a labourer at a construction site and was doing fine. But sometimes I think he sounded sad and lonely, though he did try to hide that from me. I would take the children to my neighbour's house and let them speak to their father, even though my younger daughter was just one-and-a-half and could just make sounds. The other was three and she really missed her Abbu.

Then for a long time I did not hear from him, till one day I heard rumours that he had been arrested and hauled off to jail for not possessing a proper visa or work permit. I was frantic. I didn't know what to do or whom to contact to get news about him. I was desperate to get in touch with my husband and kept asking all those who returned from these countries whether anyone had seen him or heard any news about him. But I never got a satisfactory answer. Some brushed me off as being unnecessarily worried. Others fuelled my fears by corroborating rumours about his imprisonment, and a few even suggested that it is highly likely that he has found someone else and forgotten about me.

It was then that I decided to go to Malaysia and look for him myself. My parents and siblings, other relatives, and community members told me I was crazy to try and find him on my own without the guarantee of anyone else to help. In fact, they scared me by saying that I would be raped and sold off to a brothel and my children would be taken away from me. But I was so disturbed I couldn't eat, sleep, or even think clearly. I had to find my husband.

Then one man who came to know about my desperation met me and said he would help me track him down. He said he would arrange for my trip to Malaysia and also help me find my husband. Everyone warned me that he was a trafficker and would sell me off, but this was a risk I knew I had to take. I wanted to do everything possible to find my husband.

On the cold winter morning of 26 January 2014, I boarded a boat headed for Malaysia along with my two young daughters. I took with me a small bag with a few clothes for me and my children, nothing more.

Rakhine is surrounded by the sea and I am not unused to the lurking danger of the ocean. Our camp was situated close to a port and during storms the waves would be so high we couldn't see the top of them. As a child I would cower, but as I grew older, the sea didn't scare me any more.

But nothing had prepared me for what I experienced mid-sea that day. We were packed like sardines on the boat with people spilling out of the deck and hanging by the side of the hull. My daughters were clutching on to me like they would never let go. They looked devastated. There was no food or drinking water.

Then a storm began to brew. The boat tossed and turned violently. I could see some people jumping into the water and trying to swim off, with the waves carrying them far out. Others were drowning right in front of my eyes.

I grabbed my children and held them tightly to my breast. And then the boat turned upside down. My children's grips loosened. They were carried off by the sea. All I remember after that was black water surrounding me on all sides as I slowly slipped into unconsciousness.

When I awoke I was lying on a cot on a ship whose crew had rescued me. I later learned that the ship belonged to a German shipping company based in Kolkata, India. They told me that when they found me, I, along with six other people, was holding desperately on to a floating piece of wood from a broken boat, but I have no recollection of that. My mind stopped working when my children were being swept away from me and I felt I was drowning.

When I came to my senses, I initially couldn't remember anything. Then slowly, like a painful distant memory, it all started coming back. They told me I was in shock and could not speak for days. I would just stare into space and then slip back into unconsciousness. I slept a lot.

My rescuers were very kind to me and the others, but they took more care of me as I was the only woman. They fed me and gave me clothes. For the first time in my life, I was having fruits and juices. I used to be very skinny and dark. Now, I have become fat and fair. I learned that three of the men who were rescued were from Bangladesh and have been sent back. There were two others from Myanmar, who were Rakhine Buddhists. I don't know why they were on the boat. Maybe they were going to Malaysia on some work. They too have been repatriated after the rescuers got in touch with the Myanmar government through the embassy here.

But I have not been recognized by my own country as a citizen, where my parents and relatives still live. When my memory started coming back, I could recall the phone number of one of my neighbours and contacted them. They were relieved to hear that I was alive. They told me my husband had got in touch with them while I was missing and I gave them a number here in Kolkata, India, so he could call me. He did a few times. He was devastated to hear about the death of our children. But then again the phone calls stopped. I don't know what is going on.

Since I cannot go back to Myanmar, my rescuers have kept me here. In any case, even if Myanmar wants to accept me, I refuse to go to that country. We are not even treated like humans there. And why should I go back there? My husband doesn't live there. I just want to go to my husband. I have lost my children and now all I have is him. I wish he would get in touch with me. That is all I live for.

* * *

Noor Kadir was rescued on 26 January 2014 by the crew of a ship belonging to a Kolkata-based shipping company. Since Myanmar has refused to accept her as a citizen, her rescuers have appealed to the Indian government to grant her refugee status. There has been no response yet. For the past two years, she has been living in the premises of a club belonging to the Port of Kolkata. It is a narrow room with a single bed. Her constant companion is a woman police escort. According to the shipping company, they had arranged for her to contact her parents and family in Rakhine, Myanmar. Fortunately, her husband had contacted her family in Myanmar in the meantime and the two were briefly in touch over the telephone. However, according to unconfirmed reports, though he was out on parole when he could make the phone calls, he is back in a Malaysian jail. Noor Kadir lives in the hope of being reunited with her husband one day.

—As told to Dola Mitra

This account of Noor Kadir was narrated to Dola Mitra during an interview in 2015, when the narrator was in the care of a Calcutta-based German shipping company which had rescued her after she was shipwrecked in January 2014. Her case, and legal jurisdiction, has, at the time of going to print, shifted to an international refugee body. An earlier version of this story was published in Outlook *in July 2015.*

PAKISTAN

'Our object should be peace within, and peace without.
We want to live peacefully and maintain cordial friendly relations with
our immediate neighbours and with the world at large.'

Muhammad Ali Jinnah

Pakistan hosts almost 1.4 million registered Afghan refugees—still the largest protracted refugee population globally. Between 2002 and 2015, the UNHCR had facilitated the return of 3.8 million registered Afghans from Pakistan.

The operating environment for humanitarian actors in Pakistan remains volatile, with fragile security, the problem of access, and social and economic challenges likely to affect humanitarian operations.

The main groups of people of concern include Afghan refugees—of whom approximately one-third live in refugee villages, and two-thirds in urban and rural host communities; some 7,000 asylum seekers and individually recognized refugees from various countries (mostly Afghans), living mainly in urban areas; IDPs, including those relocated by military operations and ethnic/religious conflicts in Federally Administered Tribal Areas (FATA), and, since the beginning of military operations in June 2014, IDPs from north Waziristan; and three groups presumed to be stateless or at risk of statelessness in Pakistan, namely Bengalis and Biharis from India, and Rohingyas from Myanmar.

Grief and Mistrust Walk
Hand in Hand

Rana Ram is just one of the thousands of terror-stricken Pakistani Hindus that have chosen India as a place of refuge. The Bhil Basti on the outskirts of Jodhpur in western Rajasthan that is his home now is a camp of the poorest of the poor imaginable. A majority of these refugees belong to the lowest sections of the caste and income hierarchy. Every Saturday, the Thar Link Express train brings Pakistani Hindu refugees in droves to Jodhpur. Poor and uninfluential, the refugees are twice cursed, first by radical extremism sweeping parts of Pakistan, and then upon arrival in India where border patrol and intelligence officials view them with extreme suspicion as potential Pakistani agents masquerading as aggrieved refugees.

Hindu Singh Sodha, the redoubtable volunteer and co-founder of the Pak Visthapit Sangh (Displaced Pakistanis' Organization) has for years been campaigning for the unrecognized needs of the Pakistani refugees living in Rajasthan, India. Sodha introduced me to the Bhil refugees from Pakistan that are, for now, camping in makeshift, slum-like temporary dwellings.

We are a family of 10 siblings, an equal number of brothers and sisters. All but three sisters are still in Pakistan; the rest have migrated to India. My parents live in the same tenement that I built recently in Bhil Basti.

I belong to a Bhil family from Lala Krada, a border village near Jaisalmer. Back in time, before the Partition, my grandfather went in search of work to what used to be undivided Punjab. He eventually settled in Chak Number 123 of district Rahim Yar Khan in the Punjab province. There were no borders then, so people used to venture far from their homes into areas where work beckoned. Invariably, young able-bodied men would leave behind a part of the family of elders, children, and women in the village. The bread-earners would return home at periodic intervals, their savings and goodies in tow, and after some much-needed rest, venture out again. Then, one fine day, the country was divided and my forebears found themselves deep inside the other side of the border. Hindus in a Muslim land. That's how I found myself to be Pakistani even as my ancestry, roots, and family culture lay in a border village of Rajasthan on the Indian side.

Punjab truly was a land of plenty, with enough to do for everyone, whether it was in the fields or in factories. People in large numbers must have been migrating from Rajasthan and other states of India to Punjab in search of work. Bhils, the community that I belong to, comprised at least a fourth of the village. There were other Hindu tribes as well.

In this new home in Pakistan, despite the seemingly large numbers in the village, we found the space to worship shrinking. To have a large temple built for the entire community to worship was unthinkable. So people started building small, personal temples within their courtyards in order to keep the flame of their faith alive.

I was 20 when I got married to Samdhi. She was of my age and community, from Sadiqabad, Chak Number 58. We had two children: a boy (Kailash) and a girl (Sangita). One day—just over two years into our married life—my wife was abducted by armed men, never to be returned to me again. My daughter, who was no more than three months old then, was with her mother when the incident happened.

I used to herd goats for a living, and my wife, together with my sisters and my mother, would work the cotton farms of the local landlords. Our work took us in different directions during the day. It was six in the evening when the *maulvi* descended on the fields where my wife was working, together with a bunch of local toughies and even a small posse of policemen. My mother recalls the group coming in a long row of small trucks. Samdhi's brother, Shaman, had converted to Islam only 20 days earlier after being brainwashed for months by the clerics and lured by being offered a small plot of land for building his house. Now he was a part of the maulvi's group that helped identify Samdhi as a Hindu.

The thugs wasted no time in packing away my wife in one of the waiting trucks as my mother and sisters looked on helplessly. Sangita, my three-month-old daughter, clung to her mother, so they took her as well, and overnight, they converted her to Islam. The local newspaper the following day showed Samdhi's photo, together with the maulvi, the caption indicating that she was reciting the 'Qalima' in tandem with the maulvi.

For days, I stayed enraged and helpless, not knowing what to do to bring back my wife and daughter safe from the clutches of the clerics. I filed a complaint with the village police that my wife had been picked up from the fields and forcibly made to recite the Quranic verses. Worse, they had claimed that my three-month-old daughter too had recited the verses. The court found it indefensible and decreed that the police should apprehend the culprits and that I should accompany the police to identify the wrong-doers. As it turned out, by this time the clerics had got wind of the court proceedings and made good their escape from Chak Number 58.

The judge advised that a negotiated settlement would be ideal under the circumstances. Days later, the maulvi called me to make an offer: my wife and daughter would be safely returned to me if I agreed to convert to Islam. When I refused point-blank, he retorted that it was impossible to hand me back my wife because conversion to Islam is irreversible. Then, with utmost reluctance, he agreed to have my daughter returned to me. The *faisla* was that I would keep the custody of the infant until such time that she reached an age of maturity when she would be given the option again to stay with her faith or convert to Islam.

At the farm, the Muslim landowners, who for generations had made fulsome use of the Hindu migrant labourers, started to turn hostile, holding out threats that made us shiver: 'Your days are numbered. God forbid, if there is war between India and Pakistan, you will be our first targets, make no mistake.'

At the cotton mills where I worked on daily wage, there was more than a hint of bravado and blandishments that were insistent: 'This is a nation of Muslims, don't you know that? Hindus belong to India. Either convert, or perish.'

Though my grandfather died in Chak Number 123, his advice to us was to leave and head across the border: 'The Muslims of this village will finish our faith. You must prepare to head back to India if your children must survive as Hindus. There is no future for your children here. Try everything possible to get out of here and move back to India.'

The brazenness with which they took away my wife had left me weak and vengeful. I was beginning to see a pattern emerge. I was hardly the first or the only victim of extreme intolerance. But the incident made me understand why even the poorest of the poor Hindus, those landless marginal labourers like me, had for years been fleeing Pakistan. Fear of forced conversion and the humiliation of forsaking our religion was a major factor that was forcing people to run to India. There were other reasons for the growing insecurity among our community as well: retaliation and retribution for one. Every time there was an incident of violence against Muslims in India, we saw our temples and homes burnt.

When in 1992 the Babri Masjid in the Indian town of Ayodhya was desecrated, the temples in Rahim Yar Khan were razed and looted with gay abandon. We used to sit glued to our radio sets listening to news broadcasts and reports about the maiming and killing of Hindus all over Pakistan, and temples being torched with impunity. Fear used to run through each one of us like a high-voltage current. I too did not want to stay a day longer in a land that had snatched away my wife and, with it, my peace and, happiness.

The Bhils in Rahim Yar Khan are a well-knit community even though we lived in utter penury, with not much to show for our toil and sweat of the last nearly 70 years. We were an extended family of about 150 people in my village. The community decided it was time to head back to India, whatever it took. All of them started making frantic preparations to secure a passport—almost none of us had any travel documents until then—and then to apply for an Indian travel visa. Seeing my uncles prepare to return to their homeland, I found myself thinking about the documents that I might need to cross over to India. I applied for a passport. With this, my first steps to migrate began to take shape.

My father made dozens of trips to the Indian High Commission in Islamabad to follow up on the request for visas for all of us to travel to India. After a long wait, one day he returned with the news that only four from our community were approved by the Indian embassy to travel on a short-term visa of three months. Once in India, we would have the option to apply for a longer-term stay. I learnt that I was among the members of our family cleared for travel. I received the news with much relief. But more drama was to follow.

My visa for India was nearing expiration by the time my daughter was handed back to me at the behest of the local courts. Little did the clerics or those elders who were hearing my case know that I was making preparations to leave the village, or that I had an approved visa to travel to India.

Had they known about it, I have no doubt that they would have had me killed, or, at the very least, my children kidnapped.

At last, along with my uncle, I bought a ticket for a train journey from Mirpur Khas to Munabao. From Pakistan, the Thar Express departs Karachi Cantonment every Friday at 11 p.m. and arrives at Zero Point near Khokhrapar in Pakistan at 8 a.m. on Saturday morning. After customs and visa checks, the train arrives at Munabao on the Indian side around 11 a.m. Then the passengers have to buy tickets for an Indian train called Thar Link Express, which departs at 7 p.m. and arrives at Bhagat ki Kothi in Jodhpur at 9:50 p.m. the same night. This train runs non-stop from the origin till the destination. It was a warm Saturday night when we finally arrived in Jodhpur, ragged and apprehensive but full of hope and anticipation for a future free of fear and slurs.

Alas, I was in for a surprise. The bitterness of India–Pakistan relations came back to haunt me when I had safely crossed over to the Indian side. Contrary to my expectations, the Indian officers in charge of dealing with refugees from Pakistan treated me with utmost suspicion. Every angle of my identity was scrutinized in great detail for weeks together to rule out every possibility of my being a Pakistani spy in disguise. I noticed that even women were suspects in their eyes.

Imagine the plight of a harassed person terrorized by religious bigots whose wife had been snatched away. Battling months of trauma from having faced extreme religious fundamentalism, when I arrived in Jodhpur along with my two small children, I was depressed and on the brink of a breakdown. No place to live, no money or work, and confronted by the Indian sarkari system whose hostility towards me seemed just a shade less than what I had left back in Pakistan. I was no longer sure if my decision to move out was any better than continuing my life of ignominy in Chak Number 123 in Rahim Yar Khan.

Talking to some of the other inhabitants of Bhil Basti, the unauthorized temporary settlement assigned to the arriving refugees on the outskirts of Jodhpur, I learnt that it would be a mistake to have any expectations of basic services—piped water, electricity, school for children, to name just three—being extended to me until the question of my Indian citizenship was settled. That, it turned out, could take years. There are refugees in the basti who have been living without a citizenship for 14 years or more. With all the mental agony and physical beating that I have endured, I do wonder at times if I will even be alive by the time India grants me my full rights as a citizen of this country. Will I last 14 years of further humiliation and destitution, having had my fair share of adversity even before arriving in India? If you look around in the basti you will see depression, hopelessness, and mental ailments in every person.

But life must go on. After a year-and-a-half of living in Bhil Basti, I decided to remarry, to take my mind away from my tragedies and for the joy of having a partner with whom I could start a life together. A grand-uncle in Jaisalmer mediated the alliance with Kaima, my second wife. We started our lives together, but it was not meant to last. Kaima died under mysterious circumstances while going to her parents' house when she was seven months pregnant with our first child.

A minor episode of illness presaged her untimely death. One day, she had slipped while coming back home after fetching fuel wood. Kaima complained of acute pain in the abdomen. I took her to the Umaid hospital in Jodhpur. The attending gynaecologist said the embryo had been strained. She gave her medicine for three days, and Kaima had even recovered when her father visited us and asked that his daughter accompany him back to his village, where she could rest. She passed away on the way to her parents' place. I have no clue what caused her untimely death when she seemed to have recovered from her abdominal injury during the delicate phase of pregnancy. Her father returned the next day with Kaima's body. The tradition in the community is to have the cremation and last rites of a married woman performed by her husband, and I did my best to give Kaima a fitting farewell.

And again, I am left to bring up my two children alone. Kailash is now 11 and Sangita is 9. I work in the stone quarry nearby and make 300–400 rupees (USD 4.5–6) a day. My present ordeal is to secure valid citizenship for myself and my children.

Postscript

According to Professor Satya Narain, a Jodhpur-based scholar who studies the border populations of India and Pakistan, at the time of the Partition 22 per cent of Pakistan's population was Hindu, but today it is less than 2 per cent. The size of other minority groups such as Sikhs, Buddhist, Christians, and Ahmadiyas has also shrunk in Pakistan. Christians and Ahmadiyas tend to resettle in Western countries, while Hindus and Sikhs choose India for refuge. Minorities are facing forced conversions and marriages, abductions, land grabbing, rapes, murders, kidnapping for ransom, denial of equal rights, fake blasphemy cases leading to minority settlements being set on fire and people being burnt alive, disgracing dead bodies of Hindus, and demolishing, attacking, and setting fire to Hindu temples. In 1999, Hindu Singh Sodha, together with a bunch of volunteers, founded Pak Visthapit Sangh (Displaced Pakistanis' Organization) to address the previously unrecognized needs of the Hindu Pakistani refugees living in Rajasthan, India. Sodha's mission is to advocate for the human rights of the refugees with the Indian authorities and political parties to catalyse political consensus around the issue of Hindu refugees, a majority of whom belong to the lowest sections of the caste and income hierarchy. He also works to foster a semblance of unity, hope, and kinship among the refugees through community mobilization, skills development, and income-generation activities.

SRI LANKA

'The finest island of its size in the world … the island to visit in a lifetime.'

Marco Polo

Beginning on 23 July 1983, there was intermittent insurgency in Sri Lanka against the government. This was led by the Liberation Tigers of Tamil Eelam (the LTTE, also known as the Tamil Tigers), an independent militant organization which fought to create an independent Tamil state called Tamil Eelam in the north and the east of the island. After a 26-year-long military campaign, the Sri Lankan military defeated the Tamil Tigers in May 2009, bringing the civil war to an end.

Around 80,000–100,000 people were initially estimated to have been killed during the course of the Sri Lankan conflict that lasted over 25 years.

In 2013, the UN panel estimated additional deaths during the last phase of the war to around 40,000 casualties, while other independent reports estimated the number of civilian deaths to have exceeded 100,000.

Following the LTTE's defeat, the pro-LTTE Tamil National Alliance dropped its demand for a separate state, in favour of a federal solution. In May 2010, Mahinda Rajapaksa, the then president of Sri Lanka, appointed the Lessons Learnt and Reconciliation Commission to assess the conflict between the time of the ceasefire agreement in 2002 and the defeat of the LTTE in 2009.

I Find It Hard to Heal Myself

My friendship with Vignes and Sree is another gift from Afghanistan. Over multiple seasons, as development workers by day and housemates by night, our ties prospered. Cooking, walking, and talking constituted our principal quotidian activities in a prison-like UN compound that offered little by way of meaningful diversion. Evenings and weekends were reserved for plentiful cooking and sharing stories on both sides. Though neighbours, our ignorance of our respective provincial lives, borne of limited actual contact between the north of India and its deep south, was only matched by our apparent solidarity as fellow victims of protracted political conflicts in our respective countries.

I was no more than 12 years old when I became homeless for the first time. Tragedy had struck my family even before that though, when I lost my father. I was only three then. A smart and rather successful man given his short life, my father made sure ours was a well-to-do family by the standards of those times. His early demise dealt a body blow to any dreams our parents might have nursed to give their children a happy childhood. He was a supervisor in the state shipping corporation and we lived a decent life while he was around. He passed away while on duty at the Trincomalee harbour in a freak drowning accident.

With our father gone, my mother, Easwary, graduated, almost without notice, from a young, carefree housewife into the sole caregiver, the anchor of the family, and the centre of her children's lives, and she immersed herself in the project of raising her brood of four. Life as a young widow must have been hard; discrimination and stigma attached to widowhood is commonplace in Sri Lanka. I cannot think of any other woman more dedicated to her goal of seeing through the childhood of her hapless kids. To give us a decent future, she worked, worked, and worked, until age and ill health did not permit her to take up a full-time job any more. But for years, work was all she did—in a cooperative shop, in a farm school, as a teacher in a primary school, and finally, as an assistant registrar in the Vavuniya Military Hospital.

Mother taught me to dream big and to look beyond the privations of our life. Fortunately, we did not face much humiliation as fatherless children. Our teachers were an encouraging lot and provided all the support that we needed as children of a single parent. From early on in my childhood, I worked hard to earn scholarships, which helped me complete my school and college education with flying colours.

I have no idea at what age and why I must have first nursed the dream of becoming a doctor, but I have little doubt it had a lot to do with the suffering that I was exposed to early in life.

In 1977, ours was one of the thousands of families that found itself in the crosshairs of a raging war between the Tamil guerilla groups and the Sinhalese army and the Sinhalese in almost all of the Sinhala-dominated and neighbouring districts of Sri Lanka, which led to a massive flight of Tamils from conflict-affected districts. As a result, our family had to flee from our home town, Vavuniya, to the northern neighbouring district called Kilinochchi. This was hardly the first time that I was witnessing ethnic conflict during my childhood. Since then, my entire childhood was spent in the shadow of ethnic conflict, killings, and small-and large-scale riots. The uprisings of Tamil liberation movements and excesses committed by government forces created an uncertain future for us as a minority community that was palpable everywhere in the country. The violence showed no sign of a let-up even by the 1980s. If anything, that was the time when the Tamil guerilla warfare picked up speed and sophistication, as Velupillai Prabhakaran assumed control of the dreaded LTTE. Surrounded by the incessant sound of gunfire and daily bombings, we continued our education. I entered the University of Jaffna in 1986 as a medical student. After surviving multiple disruptions and at least three major military operations, I graduated in 1994. During my internship, conflict forced me to move from the Jaffna Teaching Hospital to Pont Pedro Base Hospital and again to Kilinochchi District Hospital at the end of my internship.

The Tamils had agitated peacefully for years for equal rights. I grew up on stories of relatives and neighbours who had been a part of the protests and uprisings against the daily discrimination that our minority community was subjected to. These protests had met with little success as successive governments of the majority Sinhala leadership looked the other way when it came to meeting the legitimate demands of the Tamils. From the late 1970s, Sri Lanka had turned into a cauldron of hate, mistrust, and ethnic violence. The restive Tamils were now being led by a new set of leaders who were seeking legitimacy among the people by advocating a militant form of struggle.

As for me, after graduating in medicine, I found a job as the district medical officer of Kilinochchi and served in the district for eight years. Throughout that time, I was witness to how civilians were indiscriminately targeted by both the armed government and the opposition forces, with hospitals being constant targets.

Once, when the government forces launched a combing operation against the Tamil extremists, artillery shells fell in the hospital premises. Among those who died of injuries on the spot were two patients, a relative of a staff member who lived adjacent to the hospital, and four visitors. Eleven others, including a member of my support staff, sustained serious injuries.

The 120-bed hospital sustained massive damage in this military operation. When the district hospital had to be closed and operationally relocated to a peripheral hospital that was 20 km away from conflict zone, the bed strength was reduced to 40, with limited infrastructure and major shortage of medical supplies. Together with my small team of 11 nurses, another doctor, and three assistant medical practitioners, we managed over 1,000 outpatient cases every day. More than 100 patients—from the Kilinochchi district but also from the neighbouring districts of Mannar and Mullaitivu—needed to be admitted daily.

While we were still dealing with the aftermath of the military strikes on the hospital, we faced a major outbreak of malaria among the displaced Tamils from Jaffna. Malaria was a totally unfamiliar disease to these people who had arrived from Jaffna, the peninsular part of Sri Lanka. It was now threatening to be the single most deadly killer. On a particular day, I had to certify five deaths caused by malaria alone.

No matter how hard I try, I can never shake away the sad memories of those days. As a young doctor, I learned early on that one has to be prepared to save lives. Sub-human living conditions in the informal settlements for displaced Tamils were causing new diseases to fester, and these diseases were competing for the human toll with the daily rounds of shelling and sniper fire. Many were getting maimed due to extensive landmines that were laid out in large areas around the populated parts of Kilinochchi, Mannar, and Mullaitivu districts.

And many others were falling victim to depression and psychological trauma. A whole community was wasting away right in front of my eyes and I was unable to do much more than put my limited skills as a young doctor to use in a humanitarian crisis of epic proportions.

By 1997, as people learnt to somehow survive and carry on with their routine lives, time seemed opportune for me to reconnect with my girlfriend of many years and ask her hand for marriage. Our married life was off to a testing start. Just days after our marriage, an artillery shell dropped inside the hospital premises, less than 200 metres from our living quarters. By the year 2000, we had two kids; both had low birth weight due to a bouts of malaria that afflicted my wife during her pregnancies. Since there were no medical officers willing to take my position, I had to perforce extend my tenure in the same hospital, and she had to adapt to the setting. It was only a matter of time before the conflict would start affecting my own psychological state.

In 2002, I was sent to examine a mass grave of Tamils from the border villages of Kilinochchi district where 12 human carcasses had been found in the toilet pits in an area occupied by the Sri Lankan army. I turned depressive after this assignment and had difficulty falling asleep. No longer able to deal with such an excessive dose of human misery, in August 2003 I was able to move my family to my home town and, in 2004 I sought a transfer to my home town of Vavuniya. We started our long-desired happy life, witnessed with our third child with the birth weight of 3.4 kg, as a result of less stress and no malaria during the pregnancy.

Within months, I started receiving death threats from paramilitary groups of the Sri Lankan armed forces. They claimed that I was an LTTE sympathizer based on the fact that as a doctor I had worked in areas under LTTE control. In August 2005, the dental surgeon working with me in my private clinic was kidnapped for ransom and released after paying the amount. He told me that the group was targeting me as well. I could take it no more and started making quiet moves to get out of Vavuniya at the first opportunity. By October 2005, leaving my family behind in my home town, I had left Sri Lanka in search of a place I could call home and find some peace in.

The stress of constantly working in the conflict-affected districts, frequent threats and harassment by the paramilitary groups, and an unfulfilled inner desire to develop my career led me to migrate from my homeland to the UK, where I continued my postgraduate studies.

Due to the worsening situation back home, I made attempts to get my wife and three children to join me there, but their application was rejected by the UK immigration department. At the conclusion of my studies, I was fortunate to get a job with the World Health Organization, which was looking to hire surveillance professionals to join its Somalia programme.

After a blast incident in May 2006 near to my first two children's primary school in Vavuniya, my family took refuge in Tamil Nadu, the southernmost state of India that is just a boat ride away from Sri Lanka. I was able to move my family into a rented house in Chennai. Providing schooling to our children in private schools where they would also be well assimilated to the cultural ethos of the Tamils in India was a decisive factor that made it easy for the family to adapt to their new status as refugees in a neighbouring country. But my family was never allowed to have a bank account or any other privileges, including moving out of the country, due to their refugee status. Despite my decent professional status, decent income, standing, and UN immunity, many attempts to get a regular visa for my family in India were rejected. Meanwhile, we had our fourth child in November 2008.

I was not done with my ordeal of homelessness just yet. Once staying on in India became difficult for the family due to the restrictions in daily life, I was making plans to find a safe haven where my wife and children could live in some peace while I struggled to put bread on the table by picking some UN assignments in many of the conflict and crisis hotspots of the world that I was most suited to work in. For a while, the family joined me in Nairobi, Kenya, in May 2009. But unfortunately, I had to leave the country within three months of their arrival.

Heading back home to Sri Lanka, where, among others, my mother continued to live all by herself, was always our first option. However, the conflict had made it difficult for the internally displaced and the refugees to reclaim their homeland after so many years of homelessness. Even though the ethnic conflict had thawed somewhat, harassment and discrimination were still commonplace in many parts of the country. I decided that for the sake of our children's future, we had to find another place for our survival.

Finally, after much planning, we moved to Malaysia on education visas for my children and guardian visas for my wife and I. Malaysia offered a welcome change from our days of strife and stress as refugees. There was peace everywhere in the country. The presence of a significant number of Tamils in the country meant that our children could grow up in a cultural milieu that they could easily identify with.

It is true that as social visitors, with strict riders on our residency, we cannot purchase a house in Malaysia. The high cost of living and education—almost six times more than Sri Lanka and three times more than India—would mean that no matter how hard I worked, even a semblance of financial stability and savings would remain a distant dream.

Serving for long durations in Afghanistan and other conflict centres of the world for the UN, I continued to pay the price of staying away from my family for extended periods. This in turn put additional pressure on my wife to manage our four children almost single-handedly. Although the constraints my wife faces cannot be compared with the hardship my mother faced in the early 1970s, I have come to realize that every generation faces newer challenges. Life gets harder with each passing year. My wife used to be a strong personality who could face any difficulty that life threw at us as a family. In recent years, however, I have seen her turn emotionally fragile. Years of living and raising children as refugees has taken its toll on her.

My wife and I always dream of settling down in our homeland with our children where we live with dignity as Tamils and happiness reigns supreme. Unfortunately, our children hardly relate to Sri Lanka as their home. The modern way of living, educational scholarships, and all the creature comforts that they have been brought up on have given them a different kind of exposure. They always talk about pursuing their higher studies and even settling down in a Western country.

Displacement and the constant challenge of adapting to a new environment while dealing with the loss of our own home has left my wife and children with scars that will never heal.

Multiple migrations and the prolonged absence of a father from home has led to several psychological complications in my children's lives. My elder son, affected by internalizing problems, has ended up being out of school over one year. His troubled psychological state has left my wife and me in a state of deep despair. Despite my long years of training as a medical professional, on several occasions, I have found it hard to cope with a life filled with non-stop stress.

All my life, I have served people living in dire need of peace and basic services. Starting with my own country Sri Lanka, I went on to work in Somalia, Pakistan, South Sudan, Afghanistan, and Iraq. It is almost like I am constantly on the run trying to make a difference in one conflict-affected part of the globe or another. In all of this, I often feel my real potential as a medical professional could never be fully realized. Away from home, a protracted period of statelessness and global indifference has clearly taken its toll. Still, I wait with hope for that first dawn of peace in my life.

As Bombs Rained, Life Changed in a Jiffy

Vavuniya used to be a safe and sleepy district in northern Sri Lanka, where time stood still. I grew up in this town in a small family with my parents and two sisters. My elder sister was 12 years older than me and my younger sister was eight years my junior. My father was a man of modest means, a small businessman who had taken to full-time tailoring, a skill he had learnt as a hobby in his early years after he incurred losses in his business. With the little income my father received, we lived a happy life. During my childhood, I spent most of the time in the Murugan temple, a stone's throw from our place on 1st Cross Street, just on the fringes of town. Ours was a simple home, with only one main wall that was cemented and the other wall and roof made of tin sheets.

I studied at the Vavuniya Saiva Pragasa Vidyasalai, and spent my free time either playing with neighbourhood children or immersed in religious activities in the temple. I was good at studies and was always among the top three students at school. My ambition was to pursue engineering and become a scientist. In 1990, as I was preparing for my Grade 10 exam, also known as the 'O' levels, life changed in a jiffy.

A lot of time has passed since my first experience of homelessness—30 years to be exact. I was in Grade 5 when I first saw government forces along with Sinhalese thugs marching into Vavuniya, attacking innocent Tamil people and looting their homes. In no time, people started leaving their homes to go someplace else where they could feel safe from the military that had managed to create terror in the Tamil neighbourhoods in no time. My family, along with many others, got into the train to go to Colombo. Several other families that we knew left on the train to Jaffna. It turned out to be the last train to Jaffna until service resumed in 2014. Although it felt safe inside the train, we were still in panic mode, not knowing what fate awaited us on the way. Our fears came true when we saw one of the railway stations on our way surrounded by a group of people brandishing sticks and swords. They were screaming slogans at the top of their lungs and wore menacing looks. A fellow Tamilian on the journey said that this mob would kill all Tamils on the train. We thought this was the end for us. Some people even urinated out of fear. There must have been some good military commanders there and they ordered the troops not to allow anybody to get close to the train and attack the passengers.

Fortunately, by God's grace, the train left the station without any incidents, but the fear didn't leave us. Colombo was a long way away and we were not sure whether any incidents would happen en route or when we got down at the last station. So we were surprised when we reached Colombo safely without any untoward incident, having been prepared for the worst.

Along with two other families that we knew—there were 13 of us all together—we went to seek refuge with a family friend who was living in Elakanta, which was one-and-a-half hours away by bus from Colombo. It was a family of three—the couple and their five-year-old daughter, living in a two-bedroom rented house spread over no more than 1,000 square feet. The husband was running a small business in Colombo. It was evening, around 8 p.m., when we all arrived. They were quite surprised to see such a large group descend on to their small home without any notice.

In those days, there were hardly any telephone facilities that we take for granted these days. In any case, the conflict had left us with no option but to latch on to even the faintest source of support that we could find. I remember how this host family quickly adjusted after the initial trepidation and opened their home and hearts to us. We took over the place as if it was ours. We were served a ready supply of hot meals by the family. In turn, we contributed the little money we had to run the household.

We spent our days going to the riverbank nearby for a bath, lying for hours by the beachside, or simply walking around in the small town. There was no school for children and no jobs for adults. Life had come to a standstill. Those were the days when I started picking up some Sinhala words so as to be able to communicate with the local shopkeepers for our daily needs.

We stayed at our friend's place for two months until news came that the situation was returning to normal in Vavuniya. When we returned, it was to an open house that had been broken into and thoroughly ransacked. We found almost nothing. The little money that we had on us had almost completely run out. Before long, my father went back to his job and started earning some money. I, along with my younger sister, were enrolled back in our respective schools. After months of living a pitiful, homeless life, we were gradually getting back on our feet, and making a fresh start.

Once back at school, I worked hard to make up for lost time. I was able to keep my rank in class. Except for stray skirmishes that one got to hear of, mostly through gossip, the situation in our part of the country was showing signs of improvement. Heavy fighting was constantly being reported from Jaffna and surrounding areas, but it all seemed quite distant from where we were. Then in 1987, the Indian Peace Keeping Forces (IPKF) arrived in Sri Lanka. The radio announced that the forces had been called in to monitor the peace talks between the government and Tamil militants and also help maintain peace in the provinces in the north and east of the country. After a very long time, people there would be able to see a spell of peace in their lives.

The presence of the Sri Lankan military, long a bugbear for the Tamils, was almost non-existent. The north-east provincial council election was held for the first time, and one of the Tamil militant group leaders was elected to be a chief minister, under the direct watch of the IPKF. However, it was not too long before violence reared its ugly head, throwing our lives out of gear once again.

In the latter part of 1988, fighting resumed between one of the Tamil militant groups and the IPKF. The militant groups would settle for nothing short of a separate *eelam* (homeland) for the Tamils. They were busily recruiting school children by force, providing them with arms training, not without the tacit support of Indian forces on the ground. I started missing school and lay in hiding at home most of the time. Having seen so many young boys being taken away never to return to their homes again, I feared a similar fate might await me if I attended school.

Sometime in late 1989, the government of Sri Lanka came to an agreement with the Tamil militant groups, and together the parties to the conflict declared that the Indian troops were no longer needed and must leave the country. Once the IPKF left, the government decided to engage in peace and devolution negotiations with the Tamil militant group that was in power in the north and east. But these talks broke down even before they had started and we were back to square one. All signs pointed to a fresh standoff between the Sri Lankan military and the Tamil militant groups. The bells of war began to rumble once again.

In the meantime, those of us living in the northern and eastern parts of Sri Lanka got a good six months—January to June 1990, to be exact—when peace reigned supreme. I used this time to study for my 'O'-level examination that was scheduled for December that year. I was looking to the future with hope and much anticipation. But it all turned out to be short-lived.

It was a regular day in the second half of June that year. We had no clue that soon our lives would be turned upside down—yet again. I went to school and attended lessons as usual. Our school didn't have a parapet wall, only a barb-wire fence. There was a police station by the side of our school and a narrow road in-between. Around 10 a.m. in the morning, we saw that the police station had been surrounded by members of the Tamil militant group that was in negotiation with the government. We could not comprehend what was going on. Around 11 a.m., the school was declared closed for the day and we were asked to go home. We also saw children from other schools similarly heading towards their homes. I started running, and once home, I told my mother and the neighbourhood women about what had occurred. In the meantime, my father also came home and he informed us that all the shops and offices were also being closed.

Vavuniya was full of Tamil militants with heavy weapons. The militant group in control made an announcement that Vavuniya and its surrounding areas were under their control and local people need not live in any fear of the Sri Lankan military. A couple of nights passed without incident, but shops and schools remained closed. The quiet was breeding panic. We were all ready for the storm after the uneasy calm.

On the morning of the third day, I went to the temple, and while still there, at around 8.30 a.m., I heard huge explosions. It took just a few moments to realize that the Sri Lankan military had started indiscriminate shelling in our areas. Along with the other devotees, I took shelter behind the strong temple walls. We heard people screaming out, 'Kapaththunga kapaththunga!' ('Save me, save me!'). We peeped out of the main door of the temple and saw dead bodies lying by the roadside and some wounded people in front of the temple. We gathered courage and decided to go out and help. While we were trying to give some basic first aid to the wounded, shelling started again, so we scampered inside the temple again to take cover. In the meantime, I got the message that everybody was now making a run for it, heading out of the city, and my family was desperately searching for me. I left the safety of the temple to join my family, with just some coins for money and a handful of clothes. Through all this, the shelling had continued unabated; we came across bodies lying along our route.

The first place we went to was our distant aunt's place in Patanichur, just 5 km away from the city. By the time we reached her place, we were completely exhausted, almost on the verge of collapsing. I remember vividly being fed curry made of fresh vegetables plucked from her kitchen garden. The next week or so was spent in relative calm at her house.

The military intensified its shelling, firing rockets and pounding whole neighbourhoods. As the Sri Lankan security forces advanced, the place we had taken refuge in soon came within their artillery range and some people were killed in the neighbourhood. Again, we were on the run; this time we found shelter at a family friend's place, around 10 km from Vavuniya. When we arrived there, several displaced families like ours had already taken refuge there, and we found a corner of a room, a space that was reserved for tuitions conducted by our family friend. We stayed here for around a month, eating whatever small quantity of food was available.

After much reluctance, I took leave of my parents and decided to try my luck in Kilinochchi some 90 km away from Vavuniya, where my sister and her husband lived. With no access to any means of public transport, I bicycled all the way to Kilinochchi. A nearly 100-km bicycle ride can test the endurance levels of the best amongst us, but I was keen to escape at any cost from the incessant noise of the bombings. On the way, I found other people who were also moving to that district.

Upon reaching my sister's place, I discovered that she, who was a young mother of a month-old daughter, was pregnant with her second child. Her husband was a small farmer. The embargo imposed by the security forces on electricity, kerosene oil, and fertilizers was making it impossible for the Tamils to carry on with their farming. As days passed, people were allowed to carry things from Vavuniya only on bicycles. My brother-in-law also started going to Vavuniya, 110 km away, carrying things people needed everyday such as wheat flour, kerosene oil, sugar, coconut, and oil from there on bicycle. With the money earned from selling his wares, he bought essential supplies needed for the house, the prices of which had gone through the roof. Any income worth the name was hard to come by. My father, mother, and younger sister went back to our home and they asked me not to come back as young Tamil boys were being picked up, arrested, and killed for no reason.

I was disgusted with myself for being a burden on my sister and brother-in-law in such acutely difficult times. Although I initially helped the family by working on their small farm, I was keen to be of some tangible help to the household. With this in mind, I offered to set up shop as a street vendor to sell the things my brother-in-law brought from Vavuniya. This would help us make a better profit than was possible through selling to shopkeepers. He agreed, and I started spreading our wares by the side of the road, along with others who had had a similar idea. Soon, that corner of the street had come to resemble a small flea market. While continuing to sell things that were being brought by my brother-in-law from Vavuniya, I soon added to our small business by buying things from the local farmers. In due course, I became familiar with the tricks of buying and selling and the art of making a quick buck or two. After some weeks, as the business started expanding, I graduated to a small kiosk, a promotion of sorts from being a street vendor. Day after day, the boy who was once the best performer in his school was getting trained as a roadside vendor. This same boy who once wore a crisp white uniform to school now wore a sarong, the standard dress of his newfound profession.

Aerial attacks on places that were suspected to be used by Tamil militants for finding shelter were still common. Most of the places attacked were homes, places of worships, markets, and schools. People were always under threat. Each time we heard a plane move overhead, we would lie down on the road or under a nearby tree. Oftentimes, several planes would attack simultaneously. I know people even died out of sheer fright upon hearing the mere sound of approaching planes.

In the life that I found myself leading, I never thought that I would get an opportunity to study ever again in my life. With the passage of time, I became friends with other vendors and customers. One such customer was Niroshan, a school boy in Grade 10. One day he asked me about my past life. I described in a nutshell all that had happened and how I became a street vendor. When he heard that I was a top ranker in my school, he could not bear the thought of me continuing to be on the street selling things. He prevailed upon me to join his school and restart my studies. I only had a copy of my birth certificate, and my friend assured me that this would be adequate to get admitted to school.

I was able to save some money for one set of a school uniform and went with Niroshan to school. He spoke with his class teacher, and the three of us went to see the school principal who admitted me to the school without any hesitation.

I was only into my first week in school when we heard the booming sound of fighter planes zipping across the sky overhead. Apparently, our school was rumoured to be a target for an imminent attack. Within minutes, the children and teachers ran out and took cover in the nearby paddy fields.

While running, I fell down on the ground and injured myself. The sound of the bombs dropping in close proximity was almost heart-stopping. I remember school girls crying and running for safety. The planes dropped several bombs in the surrounding areas and left. It was an extremely frightening experience. We could not believe that we were alive. The school remained closed for the next few days.

My parents came to know about the incident and sent word through someone that the situation was getting better in Vavuniya and I should now return home. So I went back and re-joined school by the end of March 1991, during the term exams. I couldn't score well as I had been out of touch of regular studies for the past nine months. Gradually, I was able to catch up with my studies, and after wasting a whole year, I was finally able to sit for my 'O'-level exam in December 1991. I not only passed the examination this time, I actually topped in the district and enrolled on a Bachelor's degree in Business Administration. It was a four-year course, but after two years I opted out of regular classes as I had to take a job, since my father was unable to work any more.

I finished my third- and fourth-year studies while working for a government organization. Through these years of challenges, as I struggled to keep both work and studies going, I received constant encouragement from the school authorities, friends, and my teachers. I graduated in 2000. For some more time, I continued working for the same government organization but soon found a better-paying job in the corporate sector. Before long, I found myself working for a reputed international development organization. In the interim, I also managed to complete my master's in business administration and have been preparing to earn my second master's degree.

I was to learn later that in a tragic twist of fate, Niroshan, the boy who rekindled a new hope in me to join school, himself died a tragic and untimely death. In those days, when Tamil extremists were busy recruiting young, impressionable minds, my friend became enamoured by the militants' rhetoric and joined a leading Tamil militant group. He served with the group for about a year before being killed in an armed clash with the military. I also learnt that a few months later bombs were dropped on our school ground and two boys were killed and several wounded.

Although, I am settled now, my life has been filled with strange, disturbing fears. Even today, when I hear a plane fly overhead, I feel afraid. Those chilling images of aerial bombings of our neighbourhoods when death seemed just a bomb away keep rushing back. No matter how hard I try, those memories of my early days growing up in fear, poverty, and homelessness have left a pain in my heart from which I will never recover. Many of my friends and so many others lost their lives during the civil unrest in the country. Several could not continue their studies and worked for a living by taking up odd jobs. Several of them sought refugee status in India and various European countries. My dream is to have peaceful life for everyone in my country, a life where each can feel safe, respected, and equal in the eyes of the law.

Sree is not his real name. He chose not to reveal his name out of concern for his safety and that of his family.

SOUTH SUDAN

'Education of our youth, particularly girls, is necessary because you educate a girl, you empower a nation.'

Alek Wek

The world's youngest nation, South Sudan, achieved its long-awaited independence in 2011—but what should have been a cause for celebration quickly turned sour. Tensions between political and ethnic groups erupted into violence in the capital, Juba, in December 2013.

The conflict has continued to spread, reaching even the most rural areas. Now, the young country is in the grip of a massive humanitarian crisis. More than 1.8 million people are displaced in South Sudan, and another 1.4 million have fled to neighbouring countries.

Tell Them Not to Keep Me in the Camp

I met Nyethak at a government office in Addis Ababa that is charged with organizing refugee rehabilitation. As I got busy talking to a group of refugees from South Sudan, she stood on the side, unable or unwilling to talk. She had made the long journey from the faraway Gambella region of Ethiopia on the Ethiopian border with South Sudan that is now home to some 4,00,000 refugees. A vast majority of these refugees arrived into the Gambella camp that is spread over multiple settlements, following the outbreak of the ethnic conflict in South Sudan in December 2013. It took persistence and persuasion to draw Nyethak out as she spoke, haltingly, and with visible pain, about how the raging ethnic conflict in her country had consumed her husband, and turned into dust her plans to earn a degree in Ethiopia and build her career as a civil servant in the world's newest republic. Simply upended her life for good.

The South Sudanese conflict has claimed thousands of lives, and over 3.5 million South Sudanese citizens have either left the country or become internally displaced. Local insurgencies and famine have engendered a humanitarian catastrophe of monumental proportions.

The civil war was triggered by charges of coup d'etat by President Salva Kiir Mayardit against the vice president, Riek Machar.

I take my name from my parents. My mother's name was Nyethak and father's name was Koang.

It had been only a couple of months since I had arrived in Addis Ababa when fighting erupted in the winter of 2013 in Upper Nile State and led to a mass flight of our people from their homes. I had arrived there on an Ethiopian government scholarship to pursue a two-year course in civil services. The course was tailored to help me find a job in my country's government as a state bureaucrat. I remember making my way from Malakal to South Kordofan in Sudan and thence, via the border, to Addis Ababa.

I was born into a farming family and grew among three brothers and a sister. Both my parents were diligent farmers. My father loved all of his children, but when it came to me he made sure I got the best share of his time and kindness. This had, at least partly, to do with the fact that I was the eldest, but also the only one born with a disabled left leg. He always wanted to give me the comfort of being the most wanted, the most loved of his children, so that I grew up with the confidence that was needed to survive in an increasingly competitive world. It made me happy and secure as a child that, for our parents, all their children mattered a great deal and they looked after us well.

I was devastated when my father passed away. I was only 11 and all my siblings were even younger when the tragedy struck our family. Every time I think of him my heart sinks, and it makes me extremely sad to think of not having him in my life. Life is cruel. My father was a good man but he died so young, he was not even 35. Guar or Baba is what I used to call him. On the day that he passed away, the whole family was away in another village for a celebration. He wasn't ill or anything, but when we returned, he was no more. He died among the Maban people who are very different in their customs and way of life than the Nuers, the tribe that we come from. We have always suspected that he was poisoned by someone from the Mabans to settle an old score.

Mother took charge of the family and her brother pitched in with genuine solace and some financial help.

I finished high school, but my mother was keen to see me become a qualified and skilled professional. I enrolled for a three-year diploma in education and teacher training and, after graduating, soon found employment as a junior-school teacher in Nasir County in my state, a job that I held for five years.

At 20, I was married to Stephen, a man from my tribe who was also a teacher in the Upper Nile state. We have three children, the oldest is nine and the youngest is barely three. The children were all with their father when I came to Addis Ababa for the high diploma in civil services.

When the fighting erupted in Juba, the Nuer leaders called for all able-bodied youth to join the fight against the Dinka, our principal adversary. A week later, the conflict had started raging in Upper Nile, where my husband was living with our three children. Stephen arranged to cross the border with the children, leave them with me, and go back to join the fighting in our state.

Nowadays, my only connection with my homeland is through the news from the radio or TV that I manage to catch from time to time. Those arriving as refugees into the camps in Ethiopia also bring updates of the situation back home and where the latest round of bloodletting has taken people.

We all knew that the fighting was a direct consequence of the loss of power and honour felt by our leader Riek Machar. It all started when

Machar was removed by President Salwa Kiir from the position of vice president of South Sudan. Soon thereafter, as the president lost all his trust in Machar, he removed him from the position of the deputy leader of the Sudan People's Liberation Army as well, and ordered his personal security withdrawn forthwith. This was a challenge not only to Machar but a provocation to the entire Nuer community. Machar called his men to arms to give a fitting reply and save the honour of the whole community. His personal security men fought back hard.

The fighting that started in Juba on 15 December 2013 soon convulsed the whole country. Thousands of innocent men and women, young and old civilians who were unarmed and unable to fight were killed on both sides in a naked show of brutality. Hundreds of thousands fled their homes and lost their moorings forever, consigned to a life of destitution and homelessness. In village after village it seemed the tribes started mobilizing against each other. Everyone was seized by a death wish. Nuer against Dinka. Man against man.

The fighting took place from house to house and street to street, and innocent civilians and children were hacked to death in their sleep as trophies of the conflict. A countless number, a majority of them Nuer, died in Juba and Malakal. In turn, the Nuer outnumbered and outgunned the Dinka in the Nasir and Dome counties of Upper Nile, but the Dinka had the upper hand as they were better trained and armed.

In the initial days of the fighting, I was able to speak to my husband directly over the cell phone, but not for too long. Soon, however, I lost all contact with him because the mobile networks were either jammed or had been decimated in aerial bombings. It is so unfortunate how an innocent non-combatant like my husband—a mere teacher—was consigned to the flames of conflict like fat to fire. He was not inclined to be a fighter by temperament. He happened to be at the wrong place at the wrong time. That's how he got sucked into the conflict. I have no idea whatsoever if he is dead or still alive.

People abandoned their homes and hearths to escape the fires of conflict. Hundreds of thousands crossed the border and entered Ethiopia, and the government responded by setting up large refugee camps near Gambella.

Soon, I was divested of my status as a scholarship holder, and because of my South Sudanese nationality, I, along with my children, was registered as a refugee and sent to live in the Gambella camp. The USD 200 a month that I was receiving as scholarship was stopped immediately. I was told to suspend my studies and that as a refugee I was no longer entitled to the meritorious scholarship grant that I had earned to support my higher studies programme in Addis Ababa. I had to abandon the small one-room apartment that I had rented for myself and the children. But it was the sudden disruption of my studies that caused the greatest harm to my confidence. Nyatoang, my nine-year-old daughter who had started school in Addis Ababa, also had to abandon her studies. We were asked by the authorities to leave Addis and start life in the Gambella camp.

One of my abiding memories from childhood is of my parents always talking to us about the value of education. To them, good education was the only passport to a life of security and happiness. That passport stands snatched away from me and my children. This for me is the biggest downside of becoming a refugee. I have three children to raise and look after. Without the security of a decent job, I see a dark future for us.

Since I moved to the camp, there has not been a day when I have not wished to be back in Addis to complete my studies. So far I have missed out on one semester. I have been pleading with the government authorities to allow me to resume my studies. A senior official in the education department recently told me that I would be allowed to complete my studies and earn my diploma in 2017. That's a major battle won. But this reprieve is meaningless if the authorities do not let me move out of the camp.

I will knock on every door in the government to make them see reason and help me in moving out of the camp and resume my studies in Addis. That's the reason that I have chosen to leave the camp, and come back here. My children are too small to be left alone so I brought them with me and we are all camping with a close relative. It has been several days since I arrived in Addis. The relative is no longer interested in sharing his sparse accommodation with us and has been putting pressure on me to move out and look for my own shelter, wherever it may be.

With no earnings of my own, even for food I am dependent on my relatives here who hardly have enough for their own family. The UN distributes free rations among the refugees in the camp but I have had to forgo that since I returned to Addis to pursue my case for moving out of the camp.

This phase has been extremely difficult, as I have to manage my life and that of my children all by myself, without a flicker of hope of any help whatsoever from any side. I can only cry looking at my three hungry children and my own helplessness to give them even the basic sustenance they need. Can one ever get enough to eat if one is living as somebody's long-stay guest? It is not possible. Certainly not in this life of a refugee, when we live with acute shortages of every nature.

It's not easy to be weak and infirm in body and fulfil my duty as a mother at the same time. The complete lack of income and savings has drawn me to the brink of destitution. But in my heart my education helps to keep a small ray of hope alive that one day soon my future will change for the better. For that reason alone, I am not letting go of the hope that I will be allowed to complete my studies and live in Addis with some respectability, and not at anyone's mercy. And that when peace reigns in my wounded country again, I will find work in the government.

Can you tell the authorities not to tag me a refugee and consign me to a life of deprivation and hard labour in the camp? Can you tell them that for me education is everything and that I will not rest until I complete my studies?

Back home, when we got married and had a settled, secure job, my husband and I had dreams in our eyes of having a brood of children and raising a happy family. Then the conflict took over and took away from us our homes, dreams, and happiness. Today, I don't even have the satisfaction of knowing if my life partner is dead or alive, let alone having him with me.

There is no hope, but it is a small kernel of hope that keeps me alive and going.

SYRIA

'Eastward and westward storms are breaking,—great, ugly whirlwinds of hatred and blood and cruelty. I will not believe them inevitable.'

W.E.B. Du Bois, *The Wisdom of W.E.B. Du Bois*

The war in Syria has been raging for more than seven years, and there is no end in sight. Since it began in 2011, half the country's pre-war population has either died or been forced from their homes. Some remain trapped inside the country, while others have fled to neighbouring countries in search of safety.

13.5 million people in Syria need humanitarian assistance. More than 5.5 million Syrians are refugees, and 6.3 million are displaced within Syria; half are children who are at risk of becoming ill or malnourished, and being abused or exploited.

Most Syrian refugees remain in the Middle East—in Turkey, Lebanon, Jordan, Iraq, and Egypt. Inside Syria, the conditions are severe. Safety is a constant concern, as the violence continues to spread, and other basic necessities—food, water, safe shelter—are often out of reach entirely.

Who Do I Know Here?

I met Mahmoud in Izmir, Turkey's third most populous city on the western edge of a country that was flooded with refugees desperate to lunge across the Aegean Sea and cross over to Greece in the hope of making it to mainland Europe. Together with his wife and little children, he had been on the run from Aleppo in northern Syria, first making it to the ancient Turkish city of Gaziantep that is a vast home for Syrian refugees trying to escape the incessant bombardment of the Syrian regime. He was lucky enough to find work in exile as a casual wager in a daily needs store. Before long, the 12-hour shifts and soaring inflation that left him unable to afford rent and the bare essential maintenance of his family forced him to abandon his job and move onward in search of somewhat better prospects. 'I lost 12 kilos in less than a year since leaving my home in Aleppo', he told me.

Three years of a ravaged existence as a refugee, the daily desperation and slurs of a nomadic life are forcing Mahmoud to circle back to his home in Aleppo. The choices are stark. His wife is dead against taking the boat journey to the high seas to Europe and the children protest violently every time he talks about moving back to Aleppo.

Mahmoud's is one among the several accounts from Syria that I have included in this anthology. Each of these accounts speaks to an aspect of the Syrian refugee crisis—the most monumental in recent history—that is as unique as it is universal.

Since the war began in Syria in 2011, an estimated 4,00,000 Syrians have been killed. More than 5 million Syrians have fled the country and 6.3 million displaced internally.

Despite all the worries that have clouded my mind and drained my soul of all energy, I can tell you one thing for sure—that as a child, the thought that I would one day live as a refugee in a faraway, alien land with people who do not even speak my language was beyond my wildest imagination. I was like any normal kid of my age, hardly a trouble-maker. My father had a small-time job in a government department in Aleppo. None of his children had received proper schooling, let alone gone to university for higher studies. Still, peace, laughter, and happiness reigned in our house. I have only happy memories of my childhood, though life was hardly comfortable.

Where I came from, the salaries were small and families were large. Ours was no different. Like most people of their generation, my parents had nine children. Unlike children born in present times, we never thought of war and the big issues of the world. Today, if you are born in this part of the world, you are an adult almost upon arrival.

After marriage, I moved out of my parents' home in Aleppo and rented a small apartment. Most of the money I made from my small real-estate business was spent on rent and food. When the so-called revolution started, we were living in the infamous Keifak Hamra neighbourhood, which became the scene of one of Syria's most gruesome Scud missile attacks. The assault took place on 23 June 2102, in which over 186 children and adults lost their lives. All these years after the attack, my nine-year-old daughter still cannot sleep nor control her incessant crying.

Even before that attack, the area was overrun by Syrian president Bashar al-Assad's forces. Soon there were restrictions on our movements, and going to work became difficult as the regime kept the heat on the civilians through small but regular incidents of bombings.

One of my brothers who had turned a rebel fighter in Aleppo was killed in 2012 in the conflict with the government forces. He died young, and a martyr, but left a small brood of children behind. The responsibility of raising these children is a shared one among the rest of us in the family. Even as a refugee in Gaziantep, I was sending a part of my income back to Aleppo as my contribution for the maintenance of my mother, my unwed sisters, and my late brother's children.

Until that gruesome incident, I tried my best to keep my own fear at bay in order to banish any thought of moving out of the neighbourhood to a safer location. But soon after the missile incident, we left, joining thousands of others leaving their homes to a place of safety.

The whole village of Keifak Hamra emptied overnight. Almost everyone left. Men and women were walking feverishly in their pyjamas and nightclothes; they did not get the time to change. Everyone was filled with terror to the extent of not wanting to stay back even for a moment, including the closest relatives of those that died in the missile attack. Among those that reached the border village of Hraytan, a few of the youth turned volunteers and returned to Keifak Hamra the next morning to arrange for some sort of a decent burial for those who had perished in the previous day's missile attack.

Along with the unending line of pedestrians, there were thousands of cars too, ferrying families, friends, and neighbours to a place of relative safety. Close to 25,000 families, with children and few belongings, reached the village of Hrartan close to the Syrian border with Turkey. The troops of the regime were bombing the roads to keep people from leaving in such large numbers. Their real intent was to crush the revolt by holding people in siege. But people were leaving like never before.

I returned after two days to pack some of the essential items for my small children, mainly clothes, toys, and some eatables. After two days, we proceeded towards Kilis, a city on the Turkish side of the border, and we saw thousands of Syrians before us, trying to cross over. Chaos reigned everywhere. I paid off a human trafficker to get us to the other side. Luckily, it worked. From there, we took a car ride to Gaziantep, the nearest Turkish town just an hour and a half away. Upon reaching there, I was struck by the sea of Syrians; there were so many of them that for a moment I thought I was back in Syria.

In Gaziantep, I was lucky to find work within five days of arriving. The work, at a consumer goods store that dealt in kitchen appliances, silver, and tools for running a restaurant, was hard and involved long hours. For a year, I did the job without any complaints. All I wanted was a stable income to pay for the rent and my family's essential needs. It used to leave me exhausted. I lost 12 kg within one year of leaving Aleppo.

The children were growing without any sense of community, always fearful and unable to shed the terrible memories of the rain of missiles and bombs that would regularly reduce buildings and sometimes entire neighbourhoods to dust. My wife was getting more and more apprehensive about living a prolonged refugee existence in an alien land, without the support of her close relatives and friends. My 12-hour shifts at work involved lifting of heavy merchandise. A cocktail of factors finally led me to leave my job and move to Izmir in search of some stability and peace. My wife feels good about our decision to move here as she is in the midst of close relatives who had for months been imploring her to move here. It gives her solace that out here she at least has some people to talk to.

So much has happened since I left my home in Aleppo in 2012. Sitting here in Izmir today, I have hardly any energy left to think about any of the good memories. I cannot keep up any more with the daily struggles of existence, of earning enough to keep myself and my family alive. I seem to be sinking deeper and deeper into the quicksand of financial troubles. I am thinking seriously about returning to Aleppo. It will certainly be cheaper to live there in these days of withering income. At the very least, there might still be family and friends around whose sympathy and generosity one can bank upon.

Yes, in Aleppo there is a high probability of dying before my time. That is a risk worth taking if you count the difficulties of being in exile for so many years. Who do I know here? No more than two or three hapless refugee friends or relatives who, if anything, are even worse off than me. I cannot look beyond them. Back home, the common Arabic language was a strong glue that bound people together. You didn't have to know people to make new connections. Often, a warm greeting was enough to break ice with perfect strangers. In Izmir, the locals just do not like to socialize with the refugees. They all speak Turkish here. At my age, I find it tough to learn the language.

The main difficulty about living as a refugee is that although there is no war, there is no work for the refugees. Or work that gets us very little yet commits us to insanely long hours. I moved out of Gaziantep to Izmir in deference to my wife's wishes who wanted to be here because a part of her parents' family lives here, albeit in desperate conditions. But finding work has proven to be a nightmare. What upsets me no end is that I have to take help from my wife's relatives who have hardly enough for themselves.

Like each one of the refugees you meet on the streets in Izmir, I too will leave for the Greek islands as soon as I can collect the money that I need. For now, I am focused on dropping anchor in Izmir and finding myself a decent job. It is neither cheap nor easy to cross the seas, though Europe provides the hope of a safe and decent life for my children. But it costs an equivalent of USD 1,000 per person, even if one takes the most dreadful rubber dinghy, to get to the Greek islands which I hear are just 5 km away from the Izmir coast. Given the measly salaries they pay to refugees here, it will take me an entire lifetime to put away the USD 5,000 that I need for my family to make it to the boat. It's probably not going to happen any time soon.

My wife is dead against our taking to the high seas. She knows more than a thousand people have already perished in these perilous journeys and she fears for the children. On the other hand, every time I talk about moving back to Aleppo, the children protest violently. The thought of going back to the land of their worst memories traumatizes them. They don't understand that I will never be able to afford even the most basic daily needs nor pay for their education in this expensive country.

If there was even a slight hope that the war in Syria will end any time soon, I would stay put in Turkey. But there is no chance that this war will end. Not in a year, not even in 20. No chance.

My first wish is for the rain of barrel bombings in Aleppo to stop. If that happens, I will be among the first ones to move back. Even if the Turks give me a whole building here and a great salary to boot, I will still not stay a day longer than necessary. The insults and the barbs of being a refugee will never leave me.

But if the war goes on and I am condemned to live a life of perennial insults, I will pray for decent work and a salary that helps to pay my bills. I will always be a stranger here, a second-class citizen. This I have understood and accepted. Even if I speak the language and adapt well into the local environment, or live here for the rest of my life, I will not be at home.

I Crossed the Seas for My Brother

I don't remember too much about my childhood in Syria, but I think I was a happy child. My father used to say I was a good listener. I even learnt to tell stories early on and hold the attention of everyone in the house, so for my father, among all his children I was the storyteller of choice. Often, he would ask me to read his poems to guests who came over.

One day, my father sent me to his friend's house to convey his greetings. 'Say hello and shake his hand like a man not a child,' he advised me. 'He might give you a coin or something small by way of a token of love which you must accept with a smile.' I went there, as decreed by my father. There were many people in the room, including the head of the village and my uncle and aunt. I said my greetings, 'Salaam Alaikum', and shook their hands one by one. When it was my turn to shake my uncle's hand, he asked me how my father was doing. I told him, 'My father is good and he sent me here to make fun of you.' This was not polite at all, but I got away with it; I was, after all, the famous but utterly innocent five-year-old. Everyone laughed.

As a child, my mother used to say I was lucky for the family and my junior school teachers thought I was the best student. However, when I went to the next big town in the Qamishli governorate after junior school to pursue intermediate school studies, I ended up dropping a few ranks and coming sixth in class. It was around this time that I started becoming more mature as well, and began to understand life. The town was some 10 km from my village, and I studied there from grades 7 to 10. Afterwards, I went to college in Qamishli, which was even bigger for a small-town boy like me. But I was happy. For the first time, I felt I was living like a free man, in a place where everything was available. Beautiful places to visit and nice restaurants to eat in. It was a great experience. Throughout these years my parents supported me and took care of my education.

Even though I was the 10th child in the family, education was a major priority for both my parents. Each one of us finished high school at least. Only four of my siblings are still in the village. While a brother of mine lives with me here in Izmir and one of my sisters lives in Canada, I have a brother each in Algeria, the United States, Germany, and Saudi Arabia.

After completing grade 10, I joined an institute run by the Syrian ministry of education for a three-year teacher training diploma in English. Graduating as an English language teacher, I did not stop there. I registered at the University of Damascus and later in the University of Homs to major in intermediate translation. Since I had enrolled in an open-school system, I started working full-time. All along, my intention was to buy time to stay away from the mandatory military service. I am too much of a peace-loving guy to ever join the military. As a student, one is allowed to postpone military service. In early 2011, I had completed my first semester when I received an offer of employment in Algeria. To seize this opportunity, I decided to temporarily suspend my studies.

I left Syria for Algeria just a bit before the start of the war. I was still contemplating returning home to complete my studies when the war started. Somehow, it was not to be.

My father was a landlord who grew cotton on his farm. We were not rich, mainly because my father had no interest in managing his money. There were also too many mouths to feed at home.

What I learnt from being raised in a large family was that marriage is a responsibility for the future. People get married for themselves but I say we should marry for the sake of our children. If we cannot guarantee this, there is no point bringing children into this world. I have not taken the plunge as I am still in the process of feeling settled.

Before the conflict started, I used to receive job offers from a host of Gulf countries. That was a time when they used to prefer the talented and educated Syrian youth for their workforce. Once the war started in Syria, job offers started drying up. I am not interested in going abroad unless I find work there. I did not leave Syria because of the war, but to take up a job in an oil company in Algeria, where I lived from April 2011 to December 2013, when my contract ran out.

Since I was unable to return to Syria—and the authorities from the Syrian security services were looking for me there for I had not completed my military service—I decided to go to Turkey instead. The Syrian company through which I was given the job in Algeria is into contracting projects. After completing the Algerian contract, my company gave me the option to choose my next destination. I chose Turkey for two reasons—one of my brothers, Aras, was already in Izmir. He had studied music and was working as an interpreter with the International Catholic Migrants Commission (ICMC) that works for the resettlement of refugees to the US and elsewhere in North America. And I was in negotiations with an Istanbul-based British company for my next job as a safety trainer in an oil company in Erbil, Iraq.

Before taking on this new job, which looked like a sure thing, I decided to head back home for a short break. I had not been home for three years. I chose to enter Syria illegally so as to avoid facing the Syrian regime that was frantically looking for recruits for the army. It was a bit risky, but I managed to do so, and went straight to my village to spend time with my family. At the time, Turkey allowed Syrians to cross into Turkey but did not allow them to return to Syria. I took the risk and crossed into Syria from the border between the Syrian town of Qamishli and the Turkish town of Mardin. I paid my way through and thanks to the smugglers, I was able to come back. The whole journey takes about 24 hours.

At home, I was shocked to see how weak and old my father had turned during the three years that I had been away. I was used to seeing him strong, but he had changed completely. His back was bent and his voice was slow and trembling—a far cry from his once-booming baritone that would send us quivering in fright. He had become thinner. He was recovering from a heart operation that took place in Damascus. He is 85 now. My mother is the same age and, except for some knee issues, she is in good shape. Like most boys I was closer to my mother than my father.

Our father was always a distant figure in our life, a picture of gravity, and someone who my siblings never dared to cross paths with. But I broke all the borders. My brothers never smoked in front of my father, but I did it. Despite his infamous temper, I was able to talk to him openly about everything—even taboo subjects, something none of my brothers ever did. Discussion is not disrespect. Once, my father asked me to leave his house as I had turned too argumentative for his comfort. I said I would leave but that he was nevertheless wrong about the issue that was being discussed. I think he appreciated me for being outspoken. Out of respect, I would ask his forgiveness and he would forgive me easily. In our family, he is a symbol of power, while my mother, like all mothers, is a symbol of mercy and compassion.

I am a strong-willed man and known to be a decision-maker in the family, though that can be very hard to do sometimes. During my 10 days at home, I got a call from the British company that had been on the verge of making me a job offer. But the call could not go through because of poor connectivity as all mobile towers in Qamishli had been decimated. They tried to call me many times but the calls just did not go through. I could not hear anything.

I decided to quickly head back for Turkey so as to talk face-to-face with the company officials. My mother was upset and she said I should stay a bit longer as I had not been home for years. I told her that she would feel sad the day I left the house even if that happened after a year. I reasoned with her that these were troubled times and I needed work more than ever before. She understood and said a prayer for my safety and success in my world away from home.

On my way back, I paid 10,000 Syrian pounds (about USD 200) to a smuggler who helped me cross the border.

By this time, human trafficking had become a thriving business along the Turkish–Syrian borders, because of the wholesale flight of Syrians trying to escape war by crossing over to Turkey.

I crossed into Turkey via the Mardin border. From my village Bhayundur, we first went to Qamishli and then on to the border. From here the smuggler very cleverly divided us into two groups. There was just a lone border police patrol car on duty, so only one group got apprehended and turned back. Fortunately, I was in the group that couldn't be apprehended and sailed through the borders on the Turkish side, where a car was waiting for us to take us to the nearby town of Nusaybin. Next day I left for Mardin city.

I took a flight and went to Istanbul the same day; I was eager to make the most of the only job offer that I had received in a long time. As soon as I was back, I went to the office of the British company to follow up on the job offer. The company had tried to contact me the same day that I left for Syria, but unable to make contact, they selected another person as they were on a short deadline to complete the recruitment. Alas, I had lost the opportunity, the only one in three years. My brother Aras was in Istanbul at that time.

As a refugee, the first struggle is to find work that can help pay your bills. In this country, they provide medicine and healthcare for free. Nothing more. If one is not sick one does not need to avail of the free healthcare. In this country no one is recognized as a refugee. That is how the rules governing refugees are in Turkey. They call us guests, which by its nature has a 'temporary' connotation.

While in Izmir, my Syrian passport expired so I had to send it to Syria for renewal. Until such time that I get it back, I am a virtual prisoner, with no valid identity or scope to leave Turkey.

I lost the job that I had in Istanbul as the project that I was working in was not successful so the company decided to foreclose our contracts. I found a job opportunity as a translator/interpreter with an organization in Izmir, so I went there.

Izmir is quiet and peaceful but not really a city to my taste. But one thing is for certain. During my previous jobs in the oil industry, I lived in camps and deserts, now I wanted to live in a city. I am 35 and want some rest. Money is not everything. In a camp, the money is good. You save all your salary. But after work I want to go to a café and meet with friends, relax a bit.

I feel sad and sorry about the regime of discrimination that we have put in place in this world. I am a Kurd. I know what discrimination and injustice means, what loss of identity means. On my passport my nationality is mentioned as Syrian Arab. I am Kurdish, but I am not Arab; this is how the ruling Ba'ath Party characterized the Kurds to make us feel different and distant from the Syrian mainstream and possibly to keep us out of jobs or even the most basic services. There are more than 3,00,000 Kurds without a valid identity in Syria. In my job in Izmir, I met refugees from other countries, Iraqis and Afghans for example. I heard similar stories of discrimination. Only the names are different.

From time to time, I encountered an undercurrent of racism towards the refugees. Many Turks feel they are superior to others. There are all kinds of Turks in Izmir, some understanding and sympathetic, others clearly indifferent. Once, I was in a rather upscale restaurant in Izmir having a nice evening with a friend. There was a Turkish lady sitting close to us on the next table. We asked her to join us. She obliged and soon we got talking.

I was talking to my friend in English, who was translating the conversation for the lady. She seemed like a normal, agreeable woman, and happy to share her experiences of Izmir and Turkey. Everything was normal and for a while, she seemed very interested in our conversation. Towards the end, she asked where I was from. My friend, who was interpreting for both of us, told her I was from Syria. And that is when the penny dropped. In a flash she turned condescending, almost rude. She asked me what I was doing in Izmir and went on to talk disparagingly about refugees. I was shocked. Before leaving, I did tell her that since I was not her house guest and since she was not even paying for me, she did not have the right to speak to me the way she had, whether I was a Syrian or not.

She was more than 50 years of age. It was a shocking incident of racist behaviour. I told her I had been a frequent visitor to Turkey, but she retorted that I should be in Syria, fighting. I asked her if she knew about the plight of the Yezidi women at the hands of the Islamist terrorists and whether she had ever tried to put herself in their place. I told her that people do not leave their homes only because of the war; they leave because of the regular assaults on their dignity.

That encounter made me realize that these days it is almost taboo to be called a Syrian. Even the dancing girls in the cheap bars in Izmir would turn their noses when they found out you were from Syria. In order to keep the relationship normal, I refrained from revealing my Syrian identity. I sometimes become an Algerian, other times a Lebanese, and sometimes I say I am from the US.

I am a teacher, not a fighter.

I have no plans to go back to Syria, at least not any time soon. There is nothing to participate in. No work or economic activity worth the name. If there is any need to go home, I will, of course, go back.

It takes all sorts of us to make this world. Once, at the refugee welfare centre where I worked in Izmir, we were distributing UNICEF-sponsored hygiene kits for refugee children. Seeing so many children in need, a local woman who lives nearby came over with a big cake and started distributing the cake among the kids. Around the same time, another lady came and started complaining that thanks to the refugees there was too much garbage in the streets, that 'these' people were messy.

Turkey and Syria have many things in common. Even though the language is different, the food is similar. Just like Syria was before the conflict, you can find beauty everywhere in Turkey. The points of difference lie in the system of education and the culture. Most Turkish women are educated and open-minded. Syrians are more conservative. Damascus is very open, but the rest of the country not so much.

I have always been a positive person, never allowing myself to be psychologically affected by my problems. In any situation, I have the choice to be happy or sad. Yes, I am in a difficult place right now but my personal philosophy is to be positive. We get sick. Everyone gets sick. I might die. Well, everyone dies. Pain is not good but it does exist. I don't obsess too much about the problem. I try to embrace it and put my mind to work to solve the problem. We have to do what we have to do. We should be active and positive and go on.

People are running away and abandoning their homes for two reasons— security and poverty. They care about the future of their children, not so much their own present. A woman that I met recently told an American journalist to take her children to a better place and she was happy being where she was.

Those who have money cross the high seas and go to mainland Europe in search of greener pastures. Others, like me, who do not have money, look for opportunities—and shelter—closer to home.

Of course, life has a way of trumping all your plans. One day my brother Aras, who was living with me in Izmir, got a call from our father. He sounded curt and unusually firm: 'I hear you are planning to come back to Syria. My decision is that you will never come back here until the situation gets better and I give the permission to come back. This discussion is over.' Aras had chalked out many plans for his return to Syria, and he was preparing to go back by the New Year 2015. Our father's unambiguous decision put paid to all his plans.

After that call, Aras did not want to stay in Turkey any more. One day he came up to me and told me he was tired of the constant insults that he was subjected to. He said he was going to Germany, and had made up his mind to undertake the very risky voyage in crossing the sea between Turkey and Greece.

That night, Aras tried to convince me to join him on this journey; my initial response was an adamant no. When I went to bed that night, I was thinking about my parents. I asked myself what would happen if something bad happened to Aras. Being his only guardian in Turkey, I would be the one to be blamed. It was very hard for me to imagine how I would bear to see tears in my mother's eyes if, God forbid, something untoward happened to Aras during the course of the voyage.

Now, Aras is a young man full of enthusiasm and very talented. A bright future awaits him and I have always provided him support and enabled him to achieve his dreams. I did not want to be an obstacle in his way. Crossing the sea was no doubt very dangerous; many people had died while making the journey to the Greek coast, but many more had crossed successfully.

I decided that night not to leave my brother alone. I would accompany him come what may. Maybe I will not be able to do anything for him when danger strikes on the high seas, but at least I will be with him.

The next morning, I asked Aras if he was ready for the journey. He said yes, and I told him I was willing to accompany him.

We prepared for the trip, discussed all possible scenarios, and put together our travel plan. We bought personal rescue equipment from the market and made sure we had the emergency numbers of both the Turkish and Greek coastguards. And we kept our mobiles fully charged and secured them in transparent plastic bags.

And here I am now, in Giessen city in Germany, braced for a long period of uncertainty no doubt, but also looking at the future with greater hope and optimism. Who would have thought someone like me, so determined to stay put in Izmir and not court trouble by illegally crossing into Europe, would find himself in a refugee camp in Germany?

I have many plans for my future. If I have an opportunity to go anywhere better than here I too will go. The plan will change with the destination. Right now I am here.

I Will Return to Rebuild My City

It now seems like many moons ago when I used to study in a private university in a small village not far from the capital city Damascus. After spending the week at the university, I would go back to my home town, Aleppo, for the weekend. In summer I used to travel for a vacation or take an internship at an interior design studio owned by my uncle in Aleppo.

Yes, Aleppo. I don't know where to start talking about that city of my love, my birth, the one and only city in the world that I call home. It is one of the oldest continuously inhabited cities in the world. It was once known for its great architecture that had been built over centuries, perhaps even millennia. It is known to have one of the best cuisine traditions in Syria. It speaks to you in an amalgam of oriental and Mediterranean influences. Aleppans speak in their own Arabic dialect. Ours is a special culture and a friendly society.

I was 14 when the youngest of my sisters, all of whom were older than me, got married, and since then I was the only one among my siblings who was still living with my parents. Being the youngest, I was still growing up when my sisters were all getting married and leaving the house. I shared a special bond with my mother. She was my only support when I failed at the matriculation exam the first time. No matter how many times I failed in studies, her faith in my abilities remained strong as ever. She believes in me. She always has.

It was not easy for me to move away to another city to attend university as I had everything I needed when I was in Aleppo, most of all my loving parents, friends, and teachers. I have no idea what got me started on my dream to become an architect. I guess it must have had a lot to do with being surrounded by magnificent architecture in Aleppo. I was keen to complete my bachelor's degree in Syria and then pursue a master's programme in England. The plan was to then come back to Syria to start my own design and architecture firm in Aleppo with the help of my uncle, who was an established interior designer in the city. My father, a real-estate developer, had promised to support me as well. Today, that fabled Aleppo architecture lies in ruins as three-quarters of the city has been brought down by barrel bombs. If anything, when and if peace returns to Aleppo, I would be privileged to help rebuild the city of my childhood with my own two hands.

For me, the sea change that my life has gone through can be traced back to one day. It was somewhere in the middle of December 2011 when I had just completed my first semester at the undergraduate school. My friends and I were at the university, giving final touches to our final projects for the term. We looked out the windows and saw a handful of students participating in a demonstration in honour of the students who had died the previous week in Hama and Homs. Bombings by the Syrian forces targeted multiple schools and educational facilities right through the conflict, and the previous week's incident had been one of many such instances. But in a matter of minutes, the scene transformed into a battleground as the gates of the university opened and black trucks and big buses full of armed soldiers entered the campus and started physically intimidating and haranguing the protesters. The protestors—my own friends and fellow students—were packed in big trucks like cattle. What we saw was unprecedented and unbelievable. The chaos culminated with the undue harassment of screaming students and scared teachers, who were frisked and groped by the army, before their rooms were broken into and their arena of education destroyed forever.

That day, I ran away from my campus, knowing that I never wanted to be a part of this world again. A world where I could be hounded for voicing my opinion—why, just walking to class on a winter morning—was not my home. It was a place I didn't recognize. It had become a place I couldn't recognize.

Along with my childhood friend Abdul, I started to look for the easiest way for us to get out of the country. Pursuing our higher-education goals seemed to offer a way out. We applied for admission in many universities in Germany, Austria, and Switzerland. After months of waiting, we got a conditional acceptance from Vienna University of Technology in Austria. This was, of course, great news for both of us as it raised hopes of our early exit from our beloved country where violence was fast becoming a norm. We decided to move to Damascus to prepare the necessary documents. We had to travel to Beirut in Lebanon to apply for our visa because the Austrian Embassy in Damascus was closed at that time.

We applied for a student visa and then waited in Damascus with growing impatience. It was a good four months before we were called by the Austrian Embassy in Beirut to submit our passports for stamping of the visa. We went back to Aleppo and in two days booked a flight to Vienna. We packed our stuff as fast as we could. Our families and friends could hardly believe that we were leaving so soon. Our parents in particular were torn between letting us escape the dangerous and volatile situation and their need to have us close to them.

It was the first day of August 2012. Abdul hailed a taxi while I was saying goodbye to parents, my eyes full of tears, perhaps knowing that it would be a long time before we would see each other again. Finally, we were off on the long journey from Aleppo to Beirut, from Beirut to Istanbul, and then on to Vienna.

On the way to the Aleppo airport, we saw three dead bodies lying on the road by the highway. In that moment, we knew that leaving Syria was the right decision. We tried to call our parents from Istanbul during our layover at the airport there but could not get through. It was a good four days after reaching Vienna that we were able to speak to our families back in Aleppo and inform them of our safe arrival.

In Vienna, we felt like strangers in an unknown land. We were low on confidence. Not knowing anyone and not knowing our way around the new city was playing on our minds. At the same time, there was a sense of hope for the future and a feeling of safety from wanton violence. I found Vienna similar to Syria in many ways. There is a special place for customs, traditions, and music in Austrian society. I was not surprised to observe the importance of higher learning and good education in the lives of ordinary Austrians. There was also a great respect for punctuality and order and individual freedoms—values that did not resonate so well with my country.

My university in Vienna gave me one year to complete the mandatory German-language level 'B2'. It was one of the most difficult challenges of my student life. It must have been beyond my wildest imagination that one day I would have to learn German and use it in my daily life. I pushed myself to the limit to pass the language test, if only to ensure that I did not lose the opportunity to enter the university. Ten months later, I passed the examination with an impressive score. I was never more proud of myself.

I was still not sure if the university would recognize the level of my studies in Syria or if I would have to start my architecture studies all over again. This got my parents deeply worried as well. However, once I became a regular student at the university, I mustered more confidence to make enquiries about the future course of my academic life from the university authorities. One day, Abdul and I sought a meeting with the dean of the architecture department. He was very kind and had kept himself well-informed of the situation in Syria. His guidance at a critical juncture of our student life was invaluable. He understood how tough it was for us as the traumatized new migrants from Syria.

After almost one year of moving to Austria, the situation in Aleppo took a turn for the worse. My father's construction materials factory got destroyed in the war, and with it we lost our only source of livelihood. Around the same time, my father was diagnosed with intestinal cancer. He moved to Cairo, Egypt, for six months to seek better medical treatment as it was no longer possible to receive quality healthcare in Syria. The loss of income coupled with my father's failing health meant that no one could support me financially beyond the first year. I was desperate to support myself with small jobs. My student visa allowed me to work just

10 hours per week. And hardly anyone in the market was willing to hire me for such a short time.

I spent many days without food, waiting for some of my friends to invite me to have lunch together or scour newspapers and magazines for discounted food offers. I used to walk one-and-a-half hours to the university because I could not afford a ticket for any kind of public transport for two months.

Through all those difficult days, Abdul and I stayed close to each other. He stood by me through my toughest times. He would lend me money when I needed it without making me feel weak or inferior.

Knowing that it was almost impossible for me to go back to Syria, which was becoming increasingly life-threatening, together with a precarious financial situation, and having no other place or person to turn to, finally persuaded me to seek asylum in Austria. My desperate situation was getting to me—the pressure from familiarizing myself with a new language and the wholly new and unfamiliar system of studies, feeling sad and helpless because of my father's illness, and feeling lonely without my family and friends in a new country. I was fearful and apprehensive about the future. Without much work and almost penniless in a foreign land, I was falling into a state of chronic depression. This went on for about six months. I could not pass my exams at the university for a whole semester, I didn't want to go out and meet anybody, and I remained sad and felt sick most of the time. I had known that it was not going to be easy living by myself in a new country and I had been mentally prepared for it, up to a point. But there is always a difference between how we plan and how life actually shapes up for us. I expected my life to be like any ordinary person's who moves to a new country. I had thought that I would finish school and find a good job. In reality, it turned out to be way more challenging in every respect.

In general, Austrians tend to be reserved in their disposition, more so in their interactions with foreigners. It was not as easy as I had thought to strike new friendships with Austrians, perhaps because they are not that open towards people of different origins. Having an easy, extroverted personality makes me want to go out and meet new people. Back home, this helped me to build strong friendships with people from different backgrounds.

In Vienna too, I reached out to the Austrians that I met early on. It was not always easy, but I still enjoyed making new friends. I tried to frequent different meet-ups and participate in language-learning programmes to improve my German and to get to know more about the Austrian culture.

Austria is a great country with strong traditions of respect towards others, and has very strict laws against discrimination. Despite all that, every once in a while, one encounters some harassment and discrimination as an asylum seeker. Some people make it a point to remind you in different and subtle ways that you are not fully accepted. Over the years, as I built friendships and got to understand the European and Austrian culture better, I felt more at home in this beautiful country. With time, I am enjoying and appreciating living in Austria more and more.

I did not experience major incidents of racial discrimination or harassment, but I still have my fair share of small stories of facing hostile attitudes upon my arrival in Vienna. After 10 days of my arrival, when I went to renew my visa, I was asked by the person in charge at the immigration office to speak to him in German even though he was well aware that I was in a new country and needed more time to learn the local language. I observe these attitudes towards foreigners, when locals look oddly at women in headscarves, or even when we apply for jobs. My friends also believe that we are treated differently as soon as local people know that we are refugees.

I dream about travelling from one city to another, standing on the world stage in front of a great number of people, pitching and explaining new and innovative ideas and projects that I come up with to make someone's life better and easier over the next 10 years.

My goal will always be to go back to Syria when the war ends and to start projects to rebuild what has been destroyed, and be the bridge between the part of the world in which I was brought up and the part of the world where I 'grew up'.

I would like to go back to Aleppo and revive my connections with my family, relatives, and old friends, and to help the people there. To relive my childhood all over again—when there was no war and there was all the time in the world to appreciate little things. I wish the war ends soon.

I live in perpetual dread of not being able to see my parents ever again.

Beyond Successive Exiles ...

Damascus is the city where I was born and where I grew up. I did not know any other city till my mid-twenties. Like most Damascus residents, my knowledge of Syria beyond Damascus was purely touristy or based on very short business trips. Those living in the Syrian capital did not have any great curiosity to know the rest of the country. Only later did I come to know the rest of my country—thanks to my work and the revolution. Those coming to Damascus to study, work, or simply to seek a better life used to go back to visit their home towns and villages. However, the *shwwam* (original residents of Damascus) did not have any other village or city to visit. Damascus was my Syria which I rarely left. Since the city was all I had and my one and only homeland, I decided to explore it further and establish a solid relationship with it.

As soon as I attained boyhood, I began roaming every corner of my home town, drifting aimlessly from Zain El Abidine Avenue at the foot of Mount Qasioun to Al Midan Al Jouwany. I embarked on the least famous roads which lead you to the graves of the *sahaba* and saints, and to the forgotten ancient hospitals and public baths. Soon I would come to realize that all of this was an absurd attempt to possess the city. The bitter irony is that the more I got to know Damascus, the more I became alienated. I realized that the middle class, which I belong to, had been withering steadily since the early 1990s and moved gradually away from the heart of the city to live in the new modern residential suburbs on the outskirts of Damascus. I had a growing perception that the idea of homeland is really difficult to comprehend. What did it mean? What did I mean for this homeland? Was it enough to be from this land to feel a magical affiliation to this place?

Of course, these perplexing questions did not come all at once; they formalized as I gained a deeper understanding of the real map of Damascus, the one relating to influence and class, commanders and those commanded, the privileged and those living in fear, the victorious and the defeated, the nouveau riche and the impoverished. These questions took root gradually, beginning from the early 1990s, with my first encounters with children of high-ranking officers in junior high school being dropped off and picked up in their cars with tinted windows and golden numbers, with whispered conversations about children whose parents were detained or came out of detention, with me being threatened to enlist in the Ba'ath Party when I was a student wearing a loose military uniform.

I came to understand how my father and his entire generation were defeated by fear. My father was a relentless reader and a graduate from Ain Shams University in Cairo. I remember him slapping me and the blood dripping out of my lips because I talked about the influence of the intelligence services in front of our neighbour, who was certainly an informer. I was 13 years old at the time; I held back my tears and realized that fear also haunted my father. More than two decades have passed since that incident, when I had come to see my parents, both weeping like little children when they saw me entering our home after I was released from the Palestine Intelligence Branch. I looked at them with compassion. I could not say a word. I simply went to sleep, never wanting to wake up again.

I continued roaming Damascus even as an adult; however, I began to realize that this roaming was enforcing that sense of alienation that seemed fiercer the more I came to know the city and the more I realized my own vulnerability and of those like me.

Normally, the idea of vulnerability is not associated with one's homeland; it is synonymous with exile and alienation. You live in perpetual anxiety, lacking the feeling of safety and not knowing how you will continue living in that place because you cannot be part of the game of obedience and hypocrisy. You realize that your homeland is closing up on you, and that your only haven is being with people who are like you, mostly waiting for any opportunity to leave. Even if the destination is the Arabian Gulf, you work there in order to have enough money to pay to be exempted from military service, and to pay premiums for a house in a distant residential suburb. You realize how your own city is continuing to cut off all signs of hope, and how its random housing is increasing on the outskirts of the city. Thus homeland turns into exile. But I only had this homeland! It was indispensable to me. Would there ever be any salvation?

Salvation came through the creation of parallel homelands— fragmented spaces of freedom that allowed the establishment of an intimate relationship with the desired homeland. Friends in the neighbourhood and the university became a homeland—those who shared the same dreams which go beyond the walls of a homeland that almost suffocated us. We used to sit in an unobtrusive café which was then a destination for older people contemplating their solitude as they smoked the *shisha* (hookah). The café's name was Khabyny (hide me)! What were we hiding from? Was not life supposed to welcome us with open arms as befits young people in their early twenties? We convinced Abu Salim, the café owner, to allow us to smoke the light *mouassal* instead of the heavy tobacco (this achievement would benefit later generations of those hiding like us). Homeland was also present in the corridors of the Higher Institute of Dramatic Art, in the vigorous attempts to write, and in the rehearsals for completed and incomplete projects. An ancient dilapidated Damascene house near the shrine of Sheikh Muhyiddin ibn Arabi was also a homeland, where friends would meet to stay up all night and share their projects and ideas, and their love stories as well. These were miniature homelands in the middle of an overall alienation within a homeland lacking freedom. These stolen spaces of freedom are the only reason behind my nostalgia for Damascus, nothing else, not its well-known jasmine nor its hypocrisy nor its modern downtown that is choked with cement. This nostalgia casts on my soul an unbearable sadness. Nothing really tempts me to go back to that time where I was also alienated; however, nostalgia is incurable.

Many things have changed in Syria under the revolution. Unlike the time before the revolution, this is a time I long to return to, knowing obviously that it is impossible. The most beautiful thing in this totally new Syria is that I felt that I have something real to count on for the first time in my life, that my fate is linked to the fate of others around me. The exile diminished in Syria under the revolution, and features of a new homeland began to form. I regained my faith in the meaning and purpose of my existence. My new strength was not due to a particular person or group or political body; it was because of the many Syrians who, despite their different beliefs, are looking for a homeland and are fed up with exile.

In early April, at the funeral of the first martyrs from Douma, which was held in a solemn mourning tent, I was overwhelmed for the first time with an inexplicable feeling that I was not alone, that I was strong and finally had a firm grasp on the idea of belonging to a place. I quickly glanced away from the pictures of martyrs hanging on a bar at the front of the tent to meet the tearful eyes shouting loudly 'the Syrian people are one'. Few were able to hold back their tears. Those moments represented the baptism of a homeland forming before my eyes—a homeland I did not know before.

My bitter alienation at the time seemed to be crumbling in front of the mourners. My sense of belonging was consolidated more and more within the gatherings of protesters and mourners from Saqba to Al Midan and Qaboun. We were unarmed civilians in front of the sticks of the Shabiha and the bullets of the security men. However, we were very strong because it was the first time that we really wanted to live rather than die. We wanted to live in a country that was ours.

Under the revolution, our internal exile diminished with the diminution of our fear; our homeland was liberated with the liberation of our suppressed voices. In the first months of the revolution, you could sense this magical link with the idea of homeland, a voluntary and honest link. I was able to relate to the meaning of belonging, having better understood its implications; strong bonds were created among the Syrians. Even though we did not know each other or indeed have much in common, our yearning for freedom created this affiliation to a homeland, which was in the recent past an exile.

In Damascus, the distances between long-marginalized rural areas became increasingly smaller since the last decade and the city cautiously watched as the revolution sent ripples in its peripheral neighbourhoods, from Qaboun to Qudsaya. These waves of revolution did not succeed in penetrating the heart of the city, which was under tremendous military control. The struggle with fear remained fierce in Damascus, and exile continued to besiege the newborn homeland. It was then that I took the worst decision ever—to temporarily leave the country due to the security threat, hoping to come back shortly after the revolution gripped the heart of Damascus. This, of course, did not happen. I left for Beirut loaded with great dreams that quickly evaporated into thin air. Today, I realize that leaving Damascus was a tragic abortion of what seemed to be a rediscovery of a long-desired homeland. I did not know then that successive losses would come my way from that day on. I lost a long and deep love, and wonderful friends.

Away from your city, even though you were alienated there, you will lose the few things that made it possible for you to survive there. Those you left behind become angry with you because you simply left, even if they do not say so openly, while you are also angry with yourself—all the time. Others become martyrs in the cells of the intelligence system, and you, on the other hand, feel guilty because you left and could not be by their side. Those in exile have little energy to give love and tenderness, as if their souls dried up as they crossed the borders. Vacuum, like nostalgia, envelops all of you. Struggling with despair in the new exile is a strenuous task; the hardest thing about it is that individual salvation is the last resort for all those exiled.

I did not come to Beirut voluntarily; however, I chose to stay in this city (before being forced to leave). My decision to stay here was fuelled by the feeling that I was close to Syria. This closeness has various aspects to it, including that your life in Beirut moves in tandem to the rhythm of events occurring in Syria—the city swells and subsides according to the intensification of the fighting on the other side of the border. In Lebanon, you also live with tens of thousands of displaced Syrians, with the different social classes from Syria in part to Lebanon. It was bitter consolation to stay at a distance of less than a two-hour drive from Damascus. Exile in nearby countries was, until recently, a pessimistic and rejected idea. Syrians there were hoping to return soon to their homeland, the overarching thoughts being: *We are at a stone's throw. Tomorrow, things will be settled and we will return home.* These nearby places of exile seemed like temporary waiting stations before returning home, but soon you realized that they are transit stations on a longer way towards more places of exile around the globe.

In Beirut, questions about homeland and exile returned to haunt me. I was in a city that I actually loved, but it kept reminding me that I was not welcome, that I was a nobody for this city, just like its ordinary people. They were also strangers; the city was also closing up on them and their helplessness. Beirut was crushing us together, native strangers and new strangers. A city that had just come out, only ostensibly, from a devastating civil war, it still continued to feel the impact of sharp divisions. Its areas were marked with partisan or sectarian influence. Its luxurious neighbourhoods bordered its miserable cantons struggling to preserve what was left of their warm spirit, strangled by high-rise buildings forming an impregnable fence that blocked these cantons from the confiscated sea. Beirut had an inherent violence hiding in its corners, stalking its pedestrians. The city was certainly harsh on the poor, particularly the Palestinians, Syrians, and all those foreign workers, but it wasn't so merciful to its poor sons as well. For all these reasons perhaps, I understood Syria in a better way; I realized, in panic, that Lebanon is a manifestation of Syria's future.

Shortly after my arrival, I settled in the Tariq al-Jdeideh neighbourhood. I walked from there to the Sabra and Shatila camps, where Palestinians lived in abject misery and were now packed with newly displaced Syrians. Exile there means being alienated not just from your homeland but from the whole of humanity. The Palestinians who experienced exile well were now sharing their miserable living conditions with the Syrians who are now recognizing the big black hole that was threatening to engulf their dreams of returning home. After each visit, I would leave marvelling at the patience of the people living there. I would walk back through Tariq al-Jdeideh, coming down towards the Cola Bridge, past a cross line where the other side is shaded with the flags of the Amal Movement. I would pass by the

Al Janah neighbourhood with its dumb luxurious buildings, to get to the Ramlet al-Baida, where stagnant water flowed into the only free beach in the city. I would sit there with my book open but unable to read, monitoring the Syrian workers and poor people from all parts of the city trying to steal rare moments of free fun.

In Beirut, I was struggling with the idea of exile; I was once again in love with a city, even though that city did not reciprocate my love. I wanted to stay here until it was possible to return to Damascus. I regained my passion for roaming aimlessly in a city that abhors pedestrians. I changed my dwelling more than once and this helped me to understand the city better and to figure out a variety of different ways to explore it. Night roaming was my ideal way to conquer a growing insomnia.

At that time of the night, you see young people selling roses and gum, workers of late shifts in restaurants, gas stations, and parking lots sharing the night with those celebrating in bars and clubs. I would watch in amusement their faces as I crossed Mar Mikhael to Gemmaiza, then downtown to Hamra Street before passing by the lighthouse and Raouche. There I met Abu Saleh for the first time; he hailed from Soran and had been living in Aleppo. I would meet Abu Saleh more than once in the same place totally by chance, but more strangely, I met him later in a prison cell (number 9) of the Lebanese General Security Prison of Adlieh when I was arrested.

Abu Saleh was a merry and witty drunkard. For him, the whole world was a place of exile; if he returned to Aleppo he would live with the memory of his three children who were killed there, two of whom died along with their mother when an explosive barrel was thrown on their neighbourhood. However, his heart was finally and irrevocably broken after the death of his 19-year-old son, Mohamed Arab, who was killed at the hands of a sniper. He used to say a particular word whenever he described him—*khameh* (an ore). I did not understand exactly what he meant by that, but I refrained from asking him. He was a skilful narrator who could recite the Quran flawlessly. We talked about various unrelated topics, and then he would fall silent for a while and say, 'May God have mercy on him, he was a *khameh*.' Then he would ask me for money to buy alcohol. I used to leave him as he was falling asleep on the wooden chair. After coming out of the Adlieh prison, I never saw Abu Saleh again. I tried looking for him but I do not even know his real name. Abu Saleh left me believing that the entire world, including the devastated Syria, had become a place of exile for the Syrians. They were not able to return home—some didn't even have houses to return to—and they didn't know where else in the world they could find a safe haven where they could live with dignity. Countries and seas are closing to them too, and some, like Abu Saleh, are no longer willing to struggle any further.

I think of that Syrian father who was forced to throw the body of his daughter into the sea. They were on board one of the death boats heading to Italy; he was travelling for her sake, looking for an alternative homeland for both of them. She was sick with diabetes and died on the boat after the smugglers threw away the insulin package. Other passengers forced him to throw the girl's body after she died. He arrived alone in Italy.

In Beirut, and in spite of everything, I remained more capable of understanding our conditions. Not being able to understand what surrounds us is the harshest exile. I was afraid to get farther away.

In my last dwelling near Ras Beirut, one day, Ahmed, a neighbour who was in his late forties, was drunk and exhausted and shouting in the street. Neighbours gathered to rebuke him, which only caused him to shout even louder. He kept shouting until an older man convinced him to go back inside. Ahmed was a fighter in the Lebanese civil war; it was believed that he was 'capable of handling a whole block solely by himself'. The war ended but he was not good at anything else, and he had squandered his share of his family's legacy; it is rumoured that his siblings bought his property at a cheap price and left the country. He is no longer young or strong, he is no longer needed, and he does not know or understand the new Beirut. I met him once sitting on the side of the road near the entrance to the building where I lived; he was drunk but calm. He asked me to sit down, I did; he seemed so thin and old. He enquired about Syria, but did not wait for my answers. He claimed that he knew everything that was happening and what was being plotted. He was cursing everything, the regime and Hezbollah, the failure of the Arabs, and the plots of the Americans and Israelis. Finally, when there was nothing left to talk about, he leaned towards me as if disclosing a secret and said: 'War is a dirty bitch, the poor are its only victim.'

I nodded in agreement, and as I was standing up, he shouted out, 'Look at me! I'm a stranger here, a stranger in Beirut. Oh God!' I was appalled. I, the stranger, could not give him any consolation; I left him quietly. Ahmed was my gloomy conception of Syria after the war.

The last months in Beirut were a bitter struggle, made worse by the idea of forced departure. Since losing my passport and without any regular proof of residency in Lebanon, I was more vulnerable than others. Even my night roaming became more careful; I was more aware of police checkpoints and I avoided them. I spent a year-and-a half in Beirut without any legal documents. A Palestinian–Syrian friend once told me: 'The passport that enables you to travel unhindered is your only homeland.' This sounds familiar to the Palestinians in particular; the Syrian diaspora has just begun, but it simulates the Palestinian experience at a faster pace, perhaps even surpassing the Palestinian experience in terms of the number of victims and the volume of the tragedy and pain. I did not like the idea of a homeland built around a valid passport and identification papers. It seemed like a clichéd and symbolic idea. However, a life without official papers is a life where you don't have a say in almost anything, and this is also the hardest aspect of exile. The decision of the Lebanese intelligence agency, the General Security Directorate, came at the beginning of the year to change drastically the lives of Syrians living in Lebanon; tens of thousands lost their right to official residency or were in danger of losing it. This was an explicit warning that restrictions were to be imposed on the Syrians, and that they must move further away to another destination. This made it impossible for me to stay any longer in Lebanon. The General Security Directorate constantly refused to give me an official residency. The more the forced departure became inevitable, the more I got attached to Beirut. I think I preferred the places of exile that I had chosen voluntarily; I was afraid of moving to a place where expatriation became a substitute for alienation. During my last months in Beirut, I better understood the idea of living as a stranger in homelands which we love as they are. We love them simply because we do not have any other option. I was afraid of a decent life in homelands in which the only connection between us was identification papers and passports. In my last weeks in Beirut, I increased the hours of my roaming and became more inclined to isolation. I had more desire to write and love again. I became ready to do so as an act of resistance to my imminent departure. I wanted to stick to this place, but my hope and my desire was of no consequence to anyone.

At the Beirut airport, the general security officer told me with a broad smile that I was forbidden from entering Lebanon for a lifetime. For some reason this seemed funny to two young officers standing in his office! I laughed as well. And why not! The whole thing had become a comedy.

It was a good thing to arrive in Berlin during summer since the city has a gloomy winter. I was also lucky to arrive by plane; many Syrians came in miserable sea boats, or walked for months in the forests and slept in open spaces to finally reach here. Of course, exile was not what they were seeking; they were looking for an alternative homeland—a place where they could ensure a secure future for themselves and their children.

A few days ago I completed my first month here. I resort to silence most of the time, trying to comprehend my new situation in my new exile. Language is also another kind of exile. I don't know when I will begin to learn the German language. The Arabic language was also a homeland for me. I'm not good at writing in any other language. I don't want to become German or European, and even if I wanted to, I would never become one. This certainty is enough to end any conception about an alternative homeland. Here, vulnerability manifests itself in a growing sense of guilt because you live safely while your family and friends are still there at the other end of the world trapped in intensifying exiles within a burning homeland. Pondering the concept of justice in this world is a generous source of pain and alienation as well.

A friend tells me that he has become liberated from the restricting idea of homeland. He wants to roam the world, he had become tired of being captive to a desired homeland that will never be. I heard different variations on this sentence from my Syrian friends in Berlin. No doubt, it takes courage to believe this, but they all avoided looking me in the eyes while talking about being liberated from the idea of homeland and the illusions of alienation and exile. Their claimed solidity seemed like a thin cover concealing vulnerability and a combination of nostalgia to wards Syria and despair that it will never be our desired homeland. My friends and I seem like the fallen leaves of a tree, with no control over our own destinies, and not knowing exactly what their final destination will be. We only know that the wind will take us, as stated in the melancholic poem of Forugh Farrokhzad. We dream of returning to Syria. We don't know when it will happen, but until it does, perhaps we should not defy this wind. Perhaps we should carry our homelands, just like our alienation, in our hearts wherever we go.

In a State of Weightlessness

In a State of Welfaredness

'For twenty years he [Odysseus] had thought about nothing but his return. But once he was back, he was amazed to realize that his life, the very essence of his life, its center, its treasure, lay outside Ithaca, in the twenty years of his wanderings. And this treasure he had lost, and could retrieve only by talking about it ...'

—Milan Kundera, *Ignorance*

People's hearts don't care much for classifications: events, revolution, armed conflict, civil war. Minds might be bothered with these details, but not hearts. Unlike historians, ordinary people do not see historical waves heading towards stability; they are only shaken by the waves and are crushed into fragments.

The collective Syrian event was a violent rupture with the political past; however, it constitutes a deep and violent connection with the history of each individual. This is what is said and sometimes unsaid by 'citizens without identity'. Exile was an opportunity to fill in the blank spaces of their lives, which were buried in a moment and resurrected again.

The Syrians who left their Syria in the same year that I did—2014—did so for different reasons. They were from different backgrounds, of different ages, and had different stories. They spent four years under the Syrian regime's war on their country. Everyone suffered in a different way—the loss of loved ones, varying physical losses, injuries, witnessing the horrors, the chemical weapons, and collective massacres. However, they all shared a moment of exile—being forced out of their homeland, and something was confusing them all.

Those who left survived the complicity of pain and death. Their only source of horror now was not being able to be with those left behind, because they cut off the matrix of pain that defined them and left. The loved ones back home will remember the moments that created new groups, while those departing will never be part of them. If they ever came back, will they find their old places waiting for them? There is fear that their only way of defining themselves is by being associated with death. The body is also splitting apart in exile, but not in the same way it did back home; here, the body splits apart without the momentum and the red colour, it splits apart into vacuum, without memory, or let's say, without that painful desired memory.

Each one of those who left dealt with pain in their own peculiar ways. Some of them chose to wail, while others chose not to contemplate the disaster and to dismiss the desperate wailing party—and to hope. However, they were all unanimous in the belief that during the first period of exile, the only possible form of living was to live there—under the roof of death. They were accomplices of the executioner. They could only be typical victims, just as he wanted them to be. The executioner did not feel guilty enough, so they decided to take part in his heavy load. Everyone in my story feels guilty because they did not die enough. Any living that is barely a millimetre above the risk of death is an unacceptable form of living.

We went out of Syria to Lebanon before I finished my second year in college. When I decided to leave Lebanon for France, I asked my father for his opinion. My father, a man in his sixties, my idol, role model in life, and voice of reason, told me: 'Do what you see fit.' His exhausted voice and words bereft of any confidence in his own opinion broke my heart. Now for every decision that my siblings want to take, he tells them: 'Ask your sister.' He means me—a youngster in my twenties.

They say that exile is a redefinition of homeland, a means for us to reincarnate. Is it a necessary loss so that we can reshape our first identity? I cannot tell. Over the first few days in exile, I obsessively asked myself two big questions: At which moment did I decide to leave? and, Why? A magnetic force was pulling me towards death.

Why did I leave? The children, the future, and saving my own life and a few more along the way seemed to be plausible reasons. But I couldn't see any more. Actually, I did not face an imminent threat in Damascus. It was more of a political choice so as not to remain in that schizophrenic situation. When you are not able to go to the freed areas, you are practically under the regime's protection. I could not accept to stay undefined. It was obviously a problem guided by an identity crisis. I did not belong anywhere, not to the freed areas and not to Damascus under the regime. One of the honest expressions that I used to read at the beginning of the revolution without being completely aware of its implications was 'biased to the revolution'. I am one of those biased. This expression has an implied meaning: you are not the revolution. When do you *become* the revolution and not only biased to it? It is when you are dead.

I am forcibly evoking these sentences because I have forgotten why I left. Amnesia began very early in my own experience with displacement and exile. The ultimate of all losses is the loss of memory. I am addicted to memory and hostile towards time. Well, let me conjure my memories, hoping that they don't disappear or sneak in just like the rest of my life. I repeat and recount my memories like a shepherd frightened to lose one of his sheep. It is a tiresome task to guard the Museum of Memories; the more I cling to pursuing the ghosts, the more they run away from me but startle me all of a sudden. Without a form. They crawl into the limbs, cause numbness in the head. The ghosts of an afternoon scene in the Damascene heat accompanied by the sound of a prayer call from somewhere in a city that does not call for prayers.

The battle to limit the losses when you go out of your homeland is a lost one. When my daughter bumbles when saying an Arabic word, I feel something inside me is falling apart; the remainder of my strength simply slips away. It has only been a short while. Is it so easy to forget your mother tongue and homeland? This is not a question of identity or nationalistic sentiment. It is simply an estimation of the scope of the losses. When you feel that you have nothing left but language, you do not collapse because you care so much about it; in fact, you contemplate what have you actually lost *except* for language? And the comparison is not in your favour anyway. My soul falters as well at the mere idea of the possibility of no return. I pay attention to all that is said about the stories of migrants across the world and their diaspora. Which generation will return home? I spent a full semester discussing with my students some linguistic topics that are based on difficulties in translation. At the end of each discussion, they would tell me, 'Now tell us your suggestion.' I never succeeded in giving any suggestion; I manoeuvred my argument and convinced them that I only proposed the matter to introduce them to theoretical challenges. What may I propose as an equivalent to loss? When my father got out of prison, he did not come out a whole person. A part of him never returned. We may not return, just like that part.

Paris. What drives the homeless to collapse? That smell. I was haunted by the smell of the homeless for months. Smelling is older than hearing and seeing, a woman once told me. Smelling is a human's first act of bending towards the ground. I recall the smell of my mother and that of fig leaves, my first needs, the fig leaves in a dry climate in my grandmother's old house in the village. The smell. Throughout the first months of my exile, I kept dreaming that I was an outcast because of my smell. I dreamt that I was naked and defecating amid a group of people and emitting an odour. Thirty years ago, my father and his comrades were crammed in a prison in Old Damascus, where each of them had 70 cm of space. The smell must have been overwhelming in that place. When do the homeless give up and collapse? Did they come to understand something that we haven't comprehended yet? I would have collapsed if I was determined to. Since the beginning of the revolution, my father remained worried about the idea that I might get arrested. 'You can't handle prisons, you won't survive!' Who can handle prisons? Who can handle all of this havoc? I would have handled it if I was determined to. But I simply left. Now, I stare at the blanket of a homeless.

Winter 2013: Fatima was staring at the leopard-print leather blanket covering herself and her children, and wondering, *Is it possible to eat this blanket? There is nothing left that can be eaten in the whole camp.* When does a man allow himself to collapse?

My size does not suit my surroundings, just like a camel or Gulliver in the land of the Lilliputs. We are very strange; how can they understand us? These wooden floors do not seem very fixed, they must be adding to our strangeness. The houses are small, our exotic sizes are not the problem. Our nerves cannot bear all this noise, or the quiet.

When Adnan arrived in Paris, I was distraught with the realization of the gravity of our tragedy. At the beginning of the revolution, he was only 22 years old. When he left Syria, he was 26. In four years, he experienced all kinds of horrors: arrest, the siege of Douma, the chemical strike, explosive barrels, missiles, mass graves after the use of chemical weapons, the carnage following the explosive barrels. He tells his story as he smiles and laughs: 'In April 2011, I was awed to touch the body of the first martyr in Douma whose funeral procession came from the Grand Mosque in the city. After the explosive barrels, body parts meant nothing to me; the most important thing is to match the head with the right legs and to quickly bury the remains to avoid diseases and smells.'

I fidgeted with his inappropriate laughter. He held on to his laughter so as not to commit suicide. He continued with a sudden anger: 'Bombardment, aircraft, missiles, rockets, and explosive barrels are not important. They are actually nothing; you don't notice them after a while. The real horror is to get out of Douma and pass through the police checkpoints.' He remained silent for a while, then laughed again. I did not share his laughter. I asked him: 'Don't you think that you should see a psychiatrist?' 'Do you want me to wail?' he asked me instead, then carried on, 'In any case, I am much better now than I was before 2011; at least this revolution gave us the opportunity to speak. Before 2011, I did not have any hope for anything; now everything is still possible. Do you want me to wail? Many of those who are granted asylum in Europe and in the rest of the world had not suffered a bit back home; they were unharmed. Is asylum a badge of honour received by the eligible? Everything remains the same; in the past my father's salary was

1,500 Syrian pounds and all the doors were blocked; we did not belong to the opposition or to the regime and we paid the price. And we are still paying the price. I have to work unceasingly to secure resources for the besieged areas; this is the only moral justification for my being here.'

The expression 'moral justification' always appeared dozens of times in a single discussion with Adnan. He needed a moral justification in order to survive. Together, we remembered a common friend who was arrested several times during the revolution, and during his last arrest, he had to endure permanent physical damage. 'I asked him more than once to join us in Ghouta, we needed him there; he did not agree. He argued that he should stay in Damascus for political reasons. Did I not tell you that no one is willing to pay the price?'

I tried to count the number of times we repeated the word 'price'. Was it repeated more than 'moral justification'? Then I contemplated our tragedy, and recalled the text of Saeed al-Batal about people inside the siege and those outside it. I thought about my own responses—I, the one who was 'biased to the revolution', and the phrase 'one, one, one/the Syrian people are one'. I remember that autumnal evening when I failed to run into our house to warn my father of the risk of arrest. I failed to repair the damage, I failed to prevent my mother and father from becoming an offering, and I did not become an offering myself as I should have.

Exile is a treacherous tear shed without any prior planning or warning. As a police department employee held my hand to press my fingerprints on the official papers, my tears poured out immediately. The fingerprint is the ultimate and most symbolic approval of the word 'stateless' written on the passport that I used to come here. My exile is harder and more complex. I, as a Palestinian, exiled from my first exile in Syria, have to redefine the homeland from which I was exiled. I feel that Syria is my only homeland, but the revolution was a difficult test on the issue of identity. It hurts me to be asked questions such as: 'You are a Palestinian supporting the revolution? Supporting us? Excellent!' Or, 'You are Palestinian? You should mind your own business.'

I had a feeling from the very beginning that I would lose Syria. Now there are those who try to promote or are dragged behind repugnant sayings such as, 'The fate of the Palestinians in Syria is to leave the country'. If the world was able to resettle 6,00,000 Palestinian refugees outside Syria, then it can inevitably return them to Palestine.

When I was injured in 2012, 11 friends carried me to the hospital. Today, only four of them are left; the other seven are either martyrs or arrested, facing the possibility of death in prisons. Friends were always the indicators of my progress in life. I refer to them to realize that I am progressing; their outlook is an assurance of my right path. Today, I am without milestones. After Nabila's assassination in the camp last fall, I do not know who I should keep on marching on the path of life for. Nabila was my childhood friend. I thought at that if I would have to deal with the sorrow of my friend's death, it would be sometime way into the future, when we were both old. But, in fact, my problem is the past now. How can I live with all those memories? All the meanings and triumphs are not equivalent to the loss; I fool myself to avoid losses but memories startle me at every moment. Every scene, every detail, I refer to its equivalent when all those who are gone were still here. The bus, the street, the people, the trees.

In Syria, I used to manipulate language and restructure its rules as I wished; I had the freedom to do so. Now I am petrified to violate the simplest rules of the French language. How could the French citizen deduce from my French that I was a leader in my community? As a teacher, a trainer, and activist, I invested in the youth. Those in whom I invested for the future are now martyrs. How could they have known? How would I advance, and why? Maybe so that someday, I might be worthy of placing flowers on the graves of my beloved ones in the Yarmouk camp. My problem here is that memories remain in the cerebral cortex without penetrating any farther. I see a scene, it remains just that, a scene, without getting associated with rapid heartbeat or sweating or smell. This is not a memory. Perhaps this is why I cannot stand my voice any more. I no longer like to speak, I prefer to SMS people, communicating only what is necessary, and avoid long conversations.

Here, I'm undefined, not only because I'm equal to everyone in the omission of all privacy, but also because I have truncated all the signs and rituals that I mastered. My own alienation, the strange language, the helplessness, and the limited spaces are all factors that make me 'uprooted' twice; this is happening to me—the same me who was able to help numerous families in Syria every day due to the nature of my work. Now, I have to accept the guidance and assistance and mercy of those interpreting real French as it is spoken, to me.

It does not matter. I deserve and expect worse than this. I deserve to be living in the street because I left Syria. Before I left, when we were discussing the idea of the whole family leaving the country, my father's only response was, 'We left Palestine once to come to Syria. We know the meaning of exile and we will not leave our homes again except to be taken to the grave.' I understood him completely.

I did not want to admit that I was a refugee running from war. Months passed since my arrival in Paris when I finally decided to acknowledge the obvious. At first, I invested all my efforts and money in order to avoid facing this fact, in order to not be caught in a system that captures you and labels you as a refugee. But I could not continue doing so. Here, as a foreigner, it wasn't possible to gain access to normal life quickly, regardless of your level of education or financial immunity. No one would accept to rent you a dwelling; therefore, you should wait for the state to assign you an accommodation as a refugee. In all the administrative transactions which I tried to accomplish on my own, I always faced various obstacles; they make you understand that you cannot reach a conclusion because of your poor language, and that you have to rely on the social counsellor or the institutions and associations that manage the issues of the refugees.

In these departments, everything depends on the mood of the concerned persons and their interaction with you. In the end, don't they say that a large part of the problems of second-generation Moroccan immigrants to France is that the family's total dependence on the social structures weakened the symbolic authority of parents who were helpless in front of their children?

I do not want my children to live this experience. I was an important figure in my country and my community. I controlled every element of my life. Today, I panic at every detail. I am afraid that my children might not master the language quickly. I fear that they will get confused in the new school system. I fear that they will be persecuted because of their origins. I fear that they will not adapt to the new food, that they might be trapped in a loose academic system. I am fully aware that my fears are sometimes unfounded, but my anxiety stems from my feeling that I am no longer in control of anything, that I am in a state of zero gravity—weightlessness.

I deal with time in a strange way. I want to overcome all the difficulties relating to starting a new life in a new place as quickly as possible, within hours if possible. My father kept telling us that they became complete humans the minute they quit depending on the aid system and the UN Relief and Works Agency for Palestine Refugees, when they became independent and established their lives in Damascus. It seems that I am trying to shorten that period. Sixty-seven years ago, retroactively. I struggle with time to the point where I strain all those around me. I cannot bear stillness. Everyone has to be in constant motion, like the inside of a beehive. I am currently learning the new language and trying to pursue my studies; I am following up on the administrative transactions and rearing the children. What do I want to prove? And to whom? I do not know, but this is my only link with the future.

What happened in our country made us like animals sensing earthquakes—we felt what others couldn't. During the early days of my arrival, I was staring at the disaster clearly. How could all that violence accumulate only in one tiny country on the map and not affect the rest of the world? How? This is not possible. Did they not expect to be affected by the bloodbath there?

Pinar Selek, a Turkish sociologist and author, says in a small booklet on exile that before her forced exile, when she was in her home in Istanbul, she had always recited Virginia Woolf saying, 'As a woman, I have no country. As a woman, my country is the whole world'. She used to make many places her intimate home. The nature of her social struggles made her get used to roaming the streets. However, when she experienced exile, things were radically different; it was not easy at all. She resisted by trying to open the windows and doors to expand her home; to allow other winds to access her home and her soul. Will I open the doors and windows for other winds? I do not know. Now, all I know is that I will selfishly rush my children into adulthood so that I can return home.

What do you want me to say? Throughout my whole life I have not got used to saying and doing things that attract the attention of others: crying and silence. I hate to say and do things that attract the attention of others. All I can tell you is that you should rely solely on God. Leave it all to Him and trust in Him. Look! This is the same sun shining over there.

She Believed in the Unity
of Existence

My grandmother died in Damascus on 1 February 2015.

A post on Facebook informed me of her death.

She was buried the next morning. The funeral was held with those who attended. My brother, my sister, my father, my aunt, along with her husband and eldest son. I could not attend the funeral; my two uncles and their families, my aunt's youngest son, and my mother handled the burial and mourning. From our small family, my mother was able to be present and bury her mother. And she left the country a few days later.

My grandmother was the last one of my four grandparents to go. Her husband, my grandfather, died in the early eighties; I have no memories of him. On the contrary, I remember that my grandmother was always present, though she had been absent for two or three years during my early childhood years.

My grandmother did not grow a bit older since I was a child; only my mother and I grew older. Grandmothers do not grow older in the eyes of their grandchildren.

I was my grandmother's favourite grandson, or so I believed. I do not mean that she used to prefer me over the rest of her grandchildren when we were children, but that since I grew up I would visit her once or twice a week. Thus, I became the favourite and spoiled grandson. My grandmother used to make us coffee and we would sit together alone on the balcony, chattering for an hour or two.

She told me about her childhood and adolescence, her marriage and travels, and her extended family. Now, I only remember scattered parts of the oft-repeated and unrelated stories. My grandmother had a habit of shifting from one story to another, and I could never persuade her to continue her first story. As I became used to her unusual narrative style, I stopped interrupting her. I would just listen to her and drink my coffee as I reflected on Shamdeen Square below and her elegant hands.

My grandmother maintained the elegant movement of her young hands even in her eighties.

Nihad Al Haris was born to a Christian family of reasonable wealth from Homs. We do not know the exact date of her birthday, but we guess that it was in the early 1930s. My grandmother remembered her childhood house as being spacious and of genuine abundance: Arabian horses, cellars filled with food, and dozens of children having fun under the supervision of the father. My grandmother was very impressed with her mother, who died nearly 15 years ago, in 2000, when she was over 90 years old. She used to speak French and keep track of the smallest details of the family and neighbours' news. According to my grandmother, she remained good at sewing and cooking till the last days of her life. I never saw this legendary woman. My grandmother once asked to go to Homs to see her mother. But I refused, invoking flimsy reasons.

Today, I cannot remember what was so important that prevented me from getting to know my great-grandmother.

My grandmother married when she was almost 16, and moved to Hama to live with my grandfather, Michelle. The city of Hama is conservative, and she had to wear a veil whenever she wanted to go to the Muslim neighbourhoods. Soon, my grandmother became fond of the people in Hama because of their kindness, generosity, and sincerity. Later, she told me that they moved to Deir ez-Zor, where my mother was born, 'the youngest of her siblings'. My grandmother said that Deir ez-Zor was more open-minded than Hama, but she always remained nostalgic about Homs.

She felt relieved only after moving to Damascus; here, her soul found its haven in the Kurdish neighbourhood.

I try to remember some of her stories. It is late, and no one from my family is here to confirm if what I remember matches what she had told us, or matches—and this is almost impossible to confirm—reality.

My grandmother said that one of the former presidents during the 1960s had visited them in their home. She used to laugh about her confusion on that day. The president came and drank coffee in this same balcony. My grandmother was terrified and did not exchange a single word with him; she simply waited in the kitchen. She says that she should have asked him about his wife and children. When the neighbours enquired about the visit after he had left, my grandmother was forced to exaggerate the simple event: 'Yes, he was prestigious. Yes, he was smart. Of course, he was special. Oh, my husband was absolutely comfortable. Yes, yes, my husband has connections with senior officials.' She told me proudly, 'Your grandfather was not of those who are in pursuit of senior officials; he was respectable and everyone loved him.' She would remain silent for a while as if conjuring his phantom. 'God have mercy on your grandfather. I wish he knew you, my dear Odai.' She would remain silent for a long time contemplating the Damascus sky.

My grandmother told me that one of her cousins left Syria when he was seven years old. 'We had to smuggle him to Europe. Yes, he was playing with the Muslims and then they quarrelled. The Christian insulted Islam, so the Muslim gathered all his family and neighbourhood. They wanted to beat the boy badly. The incident did not subside later. So he left and never came back.' She laughed as she remembers: 'It is unbelievable how close-minded people can be! Why would anyone fight for religion?' The boy became a grandfather and lived a carefree life.

My grandmother used to tell me that the French were searching her grandfather's house looking for children to send them to school. Her grandfather refused to send his daughters. He hid the girls in the attic. However, one of them called out to the French officer and the girls went to school. The father punished the girl harshly, but eventually they were able to learn at school. My grandmother would laugh adding,

'Look how people used to think. They believed that girls don't need to learn!'

My grandmother told me that on the morning after a wedding night, the Syrians used to hang on the main door of the house the white mattress blemished with the bride's blood, as evidence of a woman's virginity on the night of the wedding. She laughed as she remembered something but she didn't tell me what it was, and said: 'How hideous this tradition is. It is good that they stopped practising it; it was a source of embarrassment for every girl.' She resumed her laughter, and I joined her, without understanding any of what she meant about the people, shame, family, and neighbours.

My grandmother dreamt that I visited her on Easter. She used to kiss me on holidays and pray for me. She laughed and told me that in her dream, I ate the full tray of *kippah* on my own, refusing to share it with anyone in the family.

'I miss you, Odai. I miss you a lot.'

I heard my uncle whispering something.

My grandmother fell into a confused silence, and whispered:

'Won't you come back to see me again?'

'Hopefully ... hopefully soon, grandma.'

During one of the holidays, I said to my grandmother that I did not believe in the resurrection of Jesus; she laughed and said: 'It does not matter what you believe, Odai, all that matters is that you are good to other people.'

My cousin was martyred by a random mortar shell coming from the Ghouta; she was newly married and still in her twenties.

Horrified by the news, I spoke to her father:

'Hello, uncle. I am Odai.'

'Who? I can't hear you.'

I repeat with the voice of the dead.

'Odai, uncle, it is Odai.'

'Oh! Hello, Odai.'

We both fell silent.

'My deepest condolences to you, uncle.'

He suddenly burst out, 'This is your freedom, Odai. This is the freedom you and your friends are pursuing. This is freedom, right? Is this freedom?'

He stopped. He was sobbing and wailing and concluded the conversation gently with heartbreaking words: 'Take care of yourself, Odai. Take care of yourself. May God protect you, may God protect you all. Take care of yourself. May God protect you. Take care of yourself for God's sake ...'

I called my grandmother the next day.

She ended the conversation after two minutes.

We couldn't find any words to say.

My grandmother had never left Syria; this is to the best of my knowledge. On Christmas and Easter, my grandmother used to drink a small cup of *araq* (a local alcoholic drink) and put on some make-up and dark lipstick. She used to celebrate with her children and grandchildren by preparing the most delicious dishes. Over decades, she kept sending us various types of food prepared by her, especially jam and *makdos*.

She always dyed her hair, and received guests with full elegance, no matter how sick she was.

My mother says that my grandmother loved life as much as she could.

My parents eloped and got married. It was what they call a *khatifh* or a runaway marriage. Her parents refused to talk to her for two or three years, before they welcomed her and her husband and children.

I asked my mother about what my grandmother did those years when she didn't communicate with her. She said that she once received a phone call but the caller did not say anything. My mother felt that the caller was my grandmother; so she cried and told her mother that she knew that it was her calling. My mother heard her mother crying on the other end. For two years or more, my mother and her mother cried silently on the phone.

I left Damascus without saying goodbye to my grandmother. I was hoping that I would visit her soon. I was afraid—and she was afraid—that she would die before I saw her again.

We both knew that I would never see her again.

All I wanted from the national unity was the freedom to visit my grandmother on Easter: between us are four years of war, the fate of being exiled hanging over my head, and the memory of her smile that heals the wounds of Jesus on the cross.

My grandmother grew suddenly older in my exile; she waited all this time to grow older behind my back. She would not have aged if I had stayed in Damascus with her. My mother returned from Beirut to Damascus to bid her goodbye. I did not speak to her as her illness intensified; I was busy studying and writing my PhD thesis and getting on with my everyday life. Maybe, I could not believe that she would really die.

My father told me that death always comes suddenly. The patient's family does not believe that their loved one will die, so death startles them, as if it never occurred to them that it was always a possibility.

'Maybe this is the nature of mankind, son. A man would go crazy if he was certain that his father, mother, or loved ones are going to die. He keeps forgetting this fact until death comes their way. Be patient and console your mother.'

My grandmother died suddenly, as all people die.

Just like Spinoza and Ibn Arabi, my grandmother believed in the unity of existence. She used to see semi-human souls in all animals. She used to feed pigeons every day on her balcony, and talk to each of her plants, telling them more tales the lonelier she became. She used to feed the turtle and say that she understood its slowness and boredom. And she used to ask the pigeons and birds to say hello to my grandfather.

My grandmother lived with her cat, whom she had named Suzy, for almost 18 years. Suzy was her best friend, and had her own chair in the living room. Suzy would stand and stare at her chair every time it was occupied by strangers. My grandmother often had to explain to her guests that that chair was the cat's chair. Suzy courted those whom my grandmother liked and attacked those she hated. When Suzy died, my grandmother was devastated, and missed her cat long after she was gone.

I left Damascus on 1 August 2011. After that, I would constantly speak to my grandmother over the phone whenever I missed her, and especially on holidays. Her voice was getting worse with time. It became mixed with sadness and bitterness.

My grandmother could not understand what happened to her country— Kurdish neighbours were protesting constantly, security was storming into the neighbourhood every week, people were being detained, some were being martyred and others turning into fugitives. Her family in Homs was displaced and dispersed between Damascus, Aleppo, Beirut, Dubai, and the West. They included detainees, informers, the silent and the confused, and those sympathetic, angry, or fearful. Those remaining in the homeland were equal in number to those in exile. Her children and grandchildren were scattered across the earth, and some of them do not even speak to each other. Television narratives revolved around stories about sectarian massacres in Homs and other Syrian cities. She spent her last days reliving memories which became mingled with the present reality, gradually swallowing everything she ever knew about her country. She became a stranger in an exile.

My grandmother died confused. Did not the 80 years she lived have any meaning, any purpose, something in which she could find peace and contentment before her departure?

With the intensification of the economic crisis in the 1980s, my grandmother used to sew some Eastern fabrics that adorn tables and sitting rooms and sell them secretly in order to contribute to the household income.

One spring day, I was sitting on the balcony with my grandmother joking as usual about matters of food and diet; she used to eat crackers and nuts all day, and suffer from obesity. She was watering her plants and talking to me and them alike. She asked me if I watched any TV series. I said that I do not watch TV; she felt sorry for me and said that actor Jamal Suleiman's new show was wonderful.

It was 9.30 a.m.

When I had come in, I had caught my grandmother preparing coffee and setting the coffee cups. I asked her about the second cup she had brought before I entered. She smiled bashfully.

My mother said that my grandmother used to drink coffee every morning with my grandfather's phantom, despite the fact that 20 years had passed since his death.

'Is it for my grandfather?' I asked.

My grandmother's face shone with an eternal youth, just like her black-and-white picture from the 1950s.

For a moment I saw my grandfather's phantom smiling at me, and then lovingly continue his contemplation of his wife.

My grandmother went to the kitchen laughing.

I remained alone on the balcony contemplating Damascus, the city of love and nostalgia, the city of fires, the city which, maybe, I will never come back to.

TIBET

'Free Tibet before free trade.'

Zhu Rongji

In 1949, the Peoples' Liberation Army of Communist China invaded Tibet. For a period of 10 years, the political and spiritual leader of this sovereign nation, His Holiness the Dalai Lama, tried to negotiate a peaceful settlement with the Chinese, but to no avail. On 10 March 1959, His Holiness was forced to leave his native land.

Following in the footsteps of His Holiness were more than 80,000 refugees. During the past 40 years, thousands of Tibetans have continued to flee their homeland and settle in various places throughout the world. India provided Tibetans with refugee status, and in the 1960s provided them some land to live on.

At great risk to their lives, Tibetans continue to leave Tibet. Parents send their children to monasteries in India with the hope that they will receive an education there and be instructed in their Buddhist religion. The Tibetan refugees and monks arrive from Tibet with absolutely nothing, requiring all essentials such as bedding, medicine, clothes, robes, and texts.

Mine to Keep the Hope Alive

In Mcleod Ganj, a town that resembles one large box of refugee stories, Kunsang is famous as the intrepid custodian of collective memories. His *Humans of Dharamshala* is a daily catalogue of ordinary Tibetans-in-exile going about their business. Being stateless and homeless in India works in different ways for different refugees. For Kunsang, life in McLeod Ganj is too soft. He feels that over the years Tibetans have become complacent and callous towards the suffering of their brothers and sisters back home in Tibet.

'Take this: back in 1997 when there was an incident of self-immolation in Tibet, the entire Tibetan diaspora in McLeod Ganj, as indeed in all the rest of the world, was on the streets filled with rage and protest against the Chinese acts of repression and denial of our legitimate rights as Tibetan citizens. We were filled with grief, anger, and protest. These days, it will take a miracle to have even a hundred Tibetans protest against acts of extreme repression meted out against our brethren. I want to make my life count for the well-being of the refugees. I dread falling into the rut of soft complacency.'

His first step was to start an NGO by the name of Tibet Hope Centre. This he did in 2008 when he was 23 and fresh out of university. For him, it has always been about keeping despondency at bay among ordinary Tibetans by lighting the torch of hope through tangible investments in skills development.

'After 30, I wanted to be my own man. I wanted to live my own dream to become a photographer and a human documentary director. In *Humans of Dharamshala*, I am finally getting to live my own dream. It's going to be one long and interesting night from here on.'

How many cups of coffee do you down every day?

It depends. If I have a lot of work, then four or five. But if it is a normal day, then one is enough.

You think coffee and work are related? Or can you separate the two?

I don't think I can. I need to be active and creative. Coffee helps me to be active, focus on this screen (pointing at the open laptop in front), and be creative. It helps me achieve all three.

Or does it? Is there no Tibetan substitute to coffee?

Oh yes, we have butter tea, but it works in the opposite direction: puts you to sleep even before you have finished your cuppa.

How about the Tibetan-style ginger–lemon–honey tea that seems to be quite the flavour in McLeod Ganj? And isn't Chinese tea supposed to be quite an elixir too?

You may be right. But it is almost like we are all moving to ape the West … sitting in a café, sipping coffee with friends seems to be the thing to do everywhere!

But speaking of staying awake and alert, one would have thought the situation of chronic homelessness would be enough to keep young and restless Tibetans up and awake all day and all night!

That's so true. I feel I am busier than others as I have decided to dive deep into community work. Still, questions about my existence as a homeless person occupy most of my mind space all the time.

So tell me more.

I am 31. I was born in Tibet and I came here when I was seven…

Sorry to break your train of thought but it just struck me that most young Tibetans that I speak to have this thing about the number seven, and even eight. They all seem to have arrived in India at that age. Can that be true or are you simply coached to say it? It seems like too much of a coincidence.

Funny, I'm hearing that for the first time. Now that you mention it, I am thinking about it. I guess by the age of six, seven, or eight we walk well. So the family decides that the child is fit to be taken to India. If you are any younger, you are a liability as you will have to be carried. And at 10, it is late for you to start your life all over again. Just my opinion.

Do you remember anything of your early life in Tibet?

When I was back home, I did not even know there was an issue between China and Tibet. Forget about India; it was nowhere in my consciousness.

That is understandable. Do you remember anything, even mundane things, from those days? What the cows looked like? The dog who barked down the street near your home? Your home? Or friends? Or school? Anything?

Yes, I do remember one thing very vividly. It did not matter if our uniform was not washed or tattered. What mattered, like life and death, was that we all wore the red ribbon pin, the symbol of the Chinese Communist Party. Also, every morning, the student assembly would start with a salute to the Chinese national flag, followed by the singing of the Chinese national anthem. I remember all this and remember my early school in Lhasa. I also remember a line of red trucks would often pass by as we clapped. They looked like fire tenders that had come to save our homes from being burnt. I was raised in Lhasa and, for the most part, by my grandparents, my three aunts, and my uncle.

What about your parents?

That opens up a raw wound as it will require me to share with you a personal story that I'd rather not remember. It's almost as though I don't have parents. When I was only a few months old, my parents separated. My twin brother went with my father and I was left in the care of my mother. As it happened, soon after the separation, my mother met a Chinese man and she took the decision to settle down with him somewhere in China. It was a difficult moment for the family, but my grandparents and my aunts made it easy for my mother by agreeing to look after me as their own. She never returned, and I never really met her.

Each one of my three aunts and my grandmother were referred to as 'ama' by me. After years and years of abandonment and not knowing the whereabouts of my real parents, I am sort of in touch with them as I found them on Facebook. I have no feelings in my heart for them though: my brother, or any of my other siblings from my parents' second marriages. Since I am an adult now, I have decided to not cling to my past nor cling to my anger about being deprived of the parental love that every child feels entitled to. I have started indulging in the hypocrisy of exchanging pleasantries with my parents and siblings. It is less because I want to do it and more because I have to do it.

My grandmother, who was everything to me, passed away several years ago in her elder daughter's house in the US. Two of my aunts live in India. I had reserves of genuine affection for my grandfather as well. One of my aunts was already in India when I took refuge here in 1992. She was the one who was insistent in her entreaties with my grandmother that I should be sent here. 'There is no future for Kunsang in Tibet,' she would implore, as I learnt later. 'All that he can be expected to learn in Tibet is the Chinese language, but if he crosses over to India, he can have a proper education. And, since I am already here, I can look after him.'

My grandparents saw the logic in this and started preparing me mentally for leaving them and travelling to India. Of course, it just did not register what it meant to leave my home. Or what or where India was. Each night my aunts would tell me stories of India and paint fancy images of a fancy country that was waiting for me with open arms. After listening to the stories, the dream to go to India had taken hold inside me and I would pester my grandmother several times a day about going there.

Unlike most people we knew, it took us just a day from Lhasa to reach the town of Dam on the Tibet–Nepal border. This was a journey others would make over a month sometimes, but we got lucky with an expert driver who was used to ferrying people from Lhasa to Dam and knew the route well. He offered to take charge of me and my aunt on the journey. That meant driving us to Dam through the shortest route and then arranging the safest way for us to cross the border into Nepal. The guy clearly had a solid network with the police and agents, which would facilitate the long and treacherous journey of Tibetans out of their own country.

There is a thriving business of people smugglers on the Tibet–Nepal border. In Dam, the driver handed us over to a guide and his wife, who exuded a reassuring air of confidence about being able to deliver us safely on the Nepalese side. Listening to them, it was clear they were quite used to moving between the two countries, and had obviously been taking people on these journeys on a daily basis. This was what they did for a living.

The guide's wife, or let's call her the junior guide, took charge of me. For most of the journey she carried me on her back as we crossed the border. Nobody knew about my presence. The woman had told me to try and fall asleep, or at least pretend I was sleeping. So I became just a piece of heavy personal load that the mountain women are accustomed to carrying over long distances. Somewhere along the way, I split from my aunt, who was a part of one of the other groups that were being accompanied by the guide. Once separated, it was not until a month had passed that I was connected with her again.

The woman who carried me on her back ran a restaurant close to the border on the Nepalese side where the locals and border patrol cops would stop by for a snack. Everyone seemed to know her. Most people also knew that the couple had two children. Once we reached her place, I was made to stay and mark time in a dingy basement barn that had a raw, wet floor and no walls. The idea clearly was to avoid raising suspicion among the cops about the presence of the third child in the house.

I recall that month spent in the barn of that Nepalese house as the worst that I ever lived through. My biggest problem was food. Until then, I had not known anything other than my own Tibetan food. Here, they served me daal–bhaat (a stew of rice and lentil soup) and it just didn't agree with my system. I would puke again and again for the first few days, refusing to accept this dietary change, a major assault on my fundamental right to eat what my palette knew to be my staple food.

The barn was just a barn, not a basement. In that dark and dank area, a busy colony of leeches and bugs gave me company. Even today, my hair stands on end thinking of those painful stings from those silent, crawling creatures all over my body. Some form of local medicine would be administered and I would get well after a few days, only to fall sick again. At the end of that month, I was pale with disease and exhaustion. I fell seriously sick with fever and swelling on my face. This time, my hosts could not manage my sickness since the place clearly lacked a qualified doctor. Even basic healthcare facilities were non-existent.

My aunt had still not reached Nepal. Or, at least, she had still not found me, and I was desperately longing to be with her. The deal clearly was that no sooner would the family arrive than I would be connected with them for our onward travel to Kathmandu, our next stop on the journey.

Kathmandu was well set up for the refugees with a proper receiving mechanism in place. My illness prompted my hosts to rush me separately— almost as an unaccompanied minor—to Kathmandu. The Tibetan Reception Centre there was equipped with basic medical facilities, lodgings, and hot Tibetan meals. Just seeing so many of my own people made me feel better. In a few days, the family also arrived, and my joy knew no bounds. Together, we headed first to Delhi and then onwards to Dharamsala and McLeod Ganj.

Coming to McLeod Ganj felt very much like home. As a child, just seeing an overwhelming number of Tibetan people in a small place was reassuring. Before long, I was admitted into the boarding school run by the Tibetan Children's Village. I so hated it initially, I could not bear the thought of being separated from the family. I did not want to be apart from my family again and here I was, having to sleep in a dorm next to a bunch of unknown children.

It was the norm to have all arriving refugee children join the school at the first opportunity. Seeing so many of the other kids in a similar situation served to soften the blow, I guess, and so, by and by, I learnt to adjust with my new life as a boarding student.

In hindsight, I have always looked back at my boarding-school days as the best that I ever lived. I often remind the current crop of children in school to enjoy this phase to the fullest, but clearly they all go through their share of discomfort and denial before they wake up to the great virtues of life in school.

I completed Grade 10 as a decent, but not exceptional, student, picking a bit of science, general awareness, and languages along the way. By the time I got admitted to college, it was getting clearer in my mind that I wanted to study arts rather than commerce or science. This was a stage when I, perhaps for the first time, became acutely aware of my Tibetan identity. Up until high school, I was only in the company of my fellow Tibetans, but college was different. All of a sudden, I was face to face with a sea of Indian boys and girls. A small percentage of Indian students would routinely heckle us for being unwelcome foreigners in their country. A strange form of revulsion was beginning to take shape inside me and I wanted to be a part of the effort to lead my community into a brighter future.

Being stateless and homeless in India works in different ways for different refugees. For me, it is an opportunity to build ourselves as people and as a community. I view life in McLeod Ganj as too soft. Over the years, we have become complacent and callous towards the suffering of our brothers and sisters back home in Tibet. Take this: Back in 1997 when there was an incident of self-immolation in Tibet, the entire Tibetan diaspora in McLeod Ganj, as indeed in all the rest of the world, was on the streets filled with rage and protest against the Chinese acts of repression and denial of our legitimate rights as Tibetan citizens. There was grief, anger, and protest. These days, it will take a miracle to have even a hundred Tibetans protest against acts of extreme repression meted out against our brethren. We, the refugees, have cornered major chunks of the donations that essentially come in the name of those that are still back home fighting against repression with their backs to the wall. It is clear to me that Tibetans in Tibet are far stronger, passionate about the cause, and more willing to fight back than those in exile. While the exiled community lives a life of dignity, in relative freedom, and fully provided with services that they need for survival, those back home continue to labour under a regime of daily harassment; this is what keeps them awake and battle-ready. I want to make my life count for the well-being of the refugees. I dread falling into the rut of soft complacency.

I completed my bachelor's in arts from St Joseph's College in Bengaluru and soon came to Dharamsala. By this time, all of my aunts and cousins had moved to the US. They asked if I wanted to join them so that they could work on preparing the necessary case documentation for my immigration. I was at a major crossroads, but it did not take me too much of an effort to decide in favour of staying back in the midst of my community in India. I thought about the invaluable investments that had been made in my education and human development for almost 20 years, all the way up to my university graduation. Now it was my turn to plough back a fraction of the care and support into constructive assistance for my fellow refugees. My own parents did not look after me the way the Tibetan refugee administration did. The Tibetan community had made those investments in me with the belief that a time would come when I would do something for Tibet. Our teachers would always remind us of our duty as the future citizens of Tibet. This was deeply embedded in my psyche and I found myself constantly trying to look for the right cause to support.

The first step was to start an NGO by the name of Tibet Hope Centre. This I did in 2008, when I was 23 and fresh out of university. For me, it has always been about working to keep despondency at bay among ordinary Tibetans by lighting the torch of hope through tangible investments in skills development. Each member of the Tibetan community in exile can improve his or her prospects by focusing on building skills that can ensure at least a decent and independent living. As long as they are unable to speak a language other than Tibetan, they will find it difficult to either set up even a small enterprise or find a small job. Inevitably, they will turn to their parents, family, and other caregivers for support. In so doing, they will create more problems for the family, and such a family can hardly be of any use to the larger struggle on behalf of the Tibetan nation. This is the start of the breakdown of the communities, and, by extension, of the nation.

I started out by offering English lessons to the exiled youth. The basic idea was that the knowledge of English would facilitate the search for a suitable job. Along the way, however, I discovered so many more problems that needed immediate attention. And I realized with each day that I am more of a social than a political activist.

I was driven by the desire to serve my community. One of the difficult issues was the isolated and lonely existence of those living in our old-age homes. These constitute the first generation of the refugees to India who came alongside or only a little after His Holiness the Dalai Lama took refuge in India in 1959. Their children, for the most part, are either still in Tibet, or happily settled in the US or elsewhere in the West. Then we have a sizeable group of youth in exile whose parents are back in Tibet. Those in the old-age homes and the youth hardly, if ever, get to see each other or relate to one another in any way. I came up with a project to bring the two groups together in order to reinforce inter-generational understanding among the exiled Tibetans and to ensure that they have a bonding of sorts.

Every now and then I visit the old-age home and I ask a student to adopt a couple. The students are not expected to make any in-cash contributions but provide psychological encouragement to the elderly. I next moved towards environment projects, and came up with a mass awareness initiative on the primacy of rivers followed by clean-up drives.

For me, work has to be fun or else I'd rather not do anything at all. Only when work is fun do we muster the energy to go to any extent to have it completed. I had done the same sort of things for eight years and I was getting a bit jaded. I needed to do something different. I had promised myself that until the age of 30, I would give my all for community development. After that, I wanted to be my own man. I wanted to live my own dream to become a photographer and a human documentary director. In *Humans of Dharamsala*, I am finally getting to live my own dream. It's going to be one long and interesting night from here on.

I Don't Know If Freedom Exists

If you enter this garment store that stands in the main square of McLeod Ganj and meet its manager, you can never believe that you are face to face with a village girl who never went to school, nor learnt to read or write. For all of life's ups and downs, I am fortunate to be alive and well.

As a peasant girl in my native Mainkung village, life was hard labour. But I would not trade it for anything. Give me my home, my cows, and my village any day over the soft and easy life of a refugee in McLeod Ganj.

The year was 1990. I was 21 years old when I, together with three other girls, set foot outside the village for the first time to get the taste of life in Lhasa, which we had heard so much about. It took us a whole month of walking 10 hours each day through the mountain passes before we got to Lhasa. The city seemed a far cry from where we had come. There were lights everywhere and tall buildings and proper asphalt roads.

We must have been in the city for no more than two or three days when my friend, Logum Tromah, and I found work as loaders of stones and cement at a construction site. It was during this time, perhaps six months or so after we arrived in Lhasa, that we came into contact with a Nepalese agent who offered to take us to India.

Now, in those days, the Tibetans in Lhasa had a palpable urge to leave Tibet to escape torture and mistreatment at the hands of the Chinese authorities that was becoming commonplace in the country. We had no money to pay the agent, although it was rather normal for Tibetans to pay their way out of the country. The agent generously allowed us to be a part of a larger group that he was escorting out of the country from the Nepalese border.

It took us a good two weeks of walking and climbing through an endless chain of mountains to reach the Tibet–Nepal border. From here, we were helped along by another Nepali guide to reach Kathmandu. The Tibetan Reception Centre in Kathmandu is a place of thriving activity. Here, we had our first shower in days.

Unkempt and weak after days and weeks of tough mountain travel, I welcomed the opportunity to wash myself. The place to stay was great too, as was the food. We stayed there for two months before we were asked to prepare ourselves for our onward journey to McLeod Ganj.

The onward journey was a breeze in comparison to what we had gone through. For a girl who had never ventured out of her village until her 20th year, I had passed through three countries in my 21st, and was looking at the prospect of settling down in a different country altogether, in a place far, far away from my village. It all seemed like a dream.

At the training centre in McLeod Ganj, run by the Tibetan government-in-exile, I enrolled for a course on carpet-weaving, and for the next 14 years, I worked at the centre as a carpet weaver. In my very first days in McLeod Ganj, while walking the streets, I met Nuwan, then a street vendor selling small Tibetan artefacts. He had separated from his first wife, but was looking after his two daughters from his first marriage. We fell in love and got married. We have three children—two daughters and a son. My eldest child, Tenzin Dadri, is 24 and pursuing her higher studies in hotel management in Switzerland. My son, the middle child, completed a one-year course in catering and is currently working as a cook with the Tibetan Reception Centre in Kolkata. My youngest daughter has gone off to Delhi to pursue her school and college studies.

A year ago, Nuwan passed away at the age of 59. Alcohol was his main enemy. Over the years, I had been watching him take to drinking like there was no tomorrow. It would start moments after he would arrive to open his shop in the morning and continue all day. We would end up fighting every night.

He would get so physical and abusive at times that I could not bear to stay in the house.

When the children would come visiting over the weekends from their boarding schools, they would all cower in terror of their father's drunken behaviour. After a point, I just couldn't take it any more. Our fights got so bad that one time I left our house to live in another village—about an hour from McLeod Ganj—in virtual anonymity. I found an Indian family willing to take me in. I just did not want to return to my husband's house, and ended up staying there for three years.

The Dalai Lama has been consistently speaking out against the rising trend of substance abuse among the exiled Tibetan youth. He has been deeply concerned about the prospect of losing a whole generation to alcoholism and drug addiction. In 1994, the sale and purchase of *chang*, the traditional Tibetan brew, was totally banned in McLeod Ganj. Going by the number of addicts I encounter on the streets each day, I doubt if the ban has worked at all. It may have gone underground, but it has not disappeared from our midst.

Wife-beating and abuse of women and children are among our greatest social evils, and these evils have been a direct consequence of excessive drinking among the refugees. Whatever their frustrations, nothing can justify the ill-treatment of women and young girls. After the burden of household chores and earning a living, the last thing we deserve is the violent treatment at the hands of our men.

As for the men, I doubt if these men can ever be a part of the struggle to return to our homeland that we so desperately long for. I thank my stars that my son does not drink even as he is surrounded by a whole generation of youngsters who indulge in all manner of substance abuse. He was so troubled by his father's excessive drinking that he has resolved not to go down that path himself. My son used to love his father deeply. He thought highly of Nuwan's skill at understanding and being able to fix gadgets and electronic items. So he felt highly let down when he saw his father lose control over his life and destiny under the influence of alcohol.

As a young girl, I did not even know that such a thing called freedom existed. Growing up in Tibet, Tibetan men and women getting beaten by the police and even Chinese thugs in plainclothes was a common sight. The slightest act of rebellion was met with great force.

I have one brother and three sisters. All but one of my siblings are still in Tibet and desperate to leave, which is becoming more and more difficult to do with each year. The Chinese government has tightened controls at the borders. They can go to any extent to keep people from leaving the country. One of my sisters got lucky and she is now in McLeod Ganj. She arrived five years ago and these days gets by selling momos on the street.

For many years now, my only link with folks back home has been through social media, WeChat being the most preferred form of communication. This is pretty much the same for all of us in exile. The Tibetans have mastered the art of small, cryptic chats, steering clear of any political conversations. The conversations typically centre around food and health. It is an open secret that all communication to and from Tibet is being closely monitored by the authorities in charge in Tibet. Far too many people have been picked up and thrown in jails on the flimsiest of grounds, having so much as casually uttered the 'P' word.

I never went to school. My mother died when I was 12, and as the eldest, I took charge of family responsibilities and started looking after my younger siblings. We come from an extremely remote village in Tibet, so remote that you wouldn't even be able to imagine it. There were no roads, electricity, or anything that you take for granted in a city these days. All my time would be spent working on the farm, herding the cattle, and preparing meals for the family. In looking after my siblings, I assumed the duties of a mother when I was just 12, years before I was married.

For me, life in exile has turned out to be decidedly less harsh. But now there is no home. There is no doubt in my mind that life was way better back in the village in Tibet that I left more than a quarter of a century ago. For one, I did not have to worry about earning money to put food on the table, or worry about having to pay house or shop rent and other bills. I live in McLeod Ganj in a cramped room and pay Rs 1,800 as monthly rent. The rent for the shop is another Rs 5,000.

Had it not been for the support that we receive from my step-daughter— my husband's daughter from a previous marriage—I would not have survived a day in exile. She is an angel. She has always considered me her own mother. Her real mother died young when this girl was too small to understand anything. It's been almost 10 years since she moved to Switzerland. She not only sponsored both my daughters for their higher education, she made sure my elder daughter also moved to Switzerland. She has made sure we all have bank accounts and makes it a point to support us financially for our major expenses.

The Dalai Lama is above all religions and preaches the way of essential humanity, the way only he can. Finding the path of love and compassion in exile are at the core of his teachings each time he sits down to address us in McLeod Ganj: 'Do not think only about yourself and your peace. There should be peace in the universe and that includes even the animal kingdom. Ask how you can walk the path of peace in the world wherever you are.' This is what he always harps upon. His undying commitment to peace rubs off on each one of us.

Across the Mountains, a Hope Called Home

When I was eight years old, I walked across the Himalayas. My mother made this decision for me, while she herself had to stay behind.

I grew up in a small, poor village in remote Tibet. It was nice there, a beautiful life, but we were very poor, and it was very hard on the villagers. At that time, my home town had no electricity, no vehicles, and not even any roads. All the houses were built by hand from mud, wood, and stone. There were also no Chinese people. But I lived there with my mother's family while she worked in Lhasa as a construction worker. They used to mistreat me, and I tried to run away on several occasions. Eventually, my mother brought me with her to Lhasa in 1996. But I couldn't stay there with her for long; there was no money and no prospects. My mother is uneducated and poor, her work as a labourer in Lhasa has no opportunities because all promotions and opportunities are offered only to the Chinese workers; Tibetan workers are shunned and ignored, treated as second-class citizens. She started working as a building labourer at the age of 20 and has great experience, but will never get any positions of seniority.

She made the decision that I had to go to India. To her, it was the only way I could get an education and a better life, free from persecution. She wanted to come with me, of course, but she couldn't afford to pay for both of us.

It cost her 2,500 yuan for a ticket for me. At the time she was earning around 500 yuan a month, so she had to take a loan.

Our journey across the Himalayas took a month and six days. It was a hard journey and many people turned back.

I met my fellow Tibetans in a deserted part of Lhasa at midnight. I was travelling with 47 strangers. Some were children and some elderly, but the majority were between the ages of 16 and 25, all searching for a better life—like me.

After half an hour of waiting in the cold, a luggage truck arrived: our transport for the next six days. The truck driver gave us some very strict advice: 'Don't make any noise. Don't get out of the truck unless I say you're in a safe place.'

We spent six days in the back of the luggage truck in complete silence. The roads were rough. We couldn't see anything outside and spent the time in constant fear of being stopped. The seats were uncomfortable and everyone was regularly sick. As the days slowly passed, everyone had migraines, travel sickness, and vomiting.

On the sixth day, we had to leave the truck to bypass security check points. The driver did try to find a way around them, but couldn't, so he returned to Lhasa, leaving us to fend for ourselves. From here on, we were on foot, facing the Himalayan mountain range.

That same night, we faced our first challenge: three fast-flowing rivers near the border on the Tibetan side. The first two we crossed fairly quickly, helped by two tall brothers who carried the luggage on their heads across the currents. Some of the bags split open and everything was lost in the water. Despite this, no one was discouraged, and the brothers helped everyone across the river. The third river was a bigger obstacle. It was swollen from the melted snow off the mountains, and very deep, with strong currents. A tall monk named Gyaltsen went first, balancing two children on his shoulders and some luggage on his back. Halfway across the river, the bag on his back fell into the river and the children and bags were washed downstream. But thankfully, the monk was a good swimmer so he finally rescued the children as well as the bag and crossed the river.

Gyaltsen was the strongest swimmer, and although we all tried, walking up and down beside the river to find a narrower point, we couldn't cross it that night. After a day, the river swell decreased, and eventually we all made it through the freezing waters to the other side.

To avoid detection by the Chinese, we slept during the day and walked at night. It was exhausting, and several of the older Tibetans chose to turn back and return home. I was too weak to even carry an empty bag; every step was a struggle. I felt sleepy all the time. We walked through sparse forests; sharp thistles got stuck to all of our clothes, scratching our skin through the material. We had to stop often to pull them off.

We had been walking for 25 days when we encountered our first bout of food and water shortage. Things were looking dire. We had some cash, but being in such remote countryside, there were no shops to buy anything from. Between us and our destination of Nepal were seven huge mountain ranges. It took two full days to cross them, walking through thick ice and snow.

We ran into other problems in those mountains. The blinding white reflections of the snow burned our eyes, and the snow itself burned our skin. One man's hip was burned so badly that he got severe frostbite and his leg had to be amputated. Another child also got frostbite in his fingers, which also had to be amputated.

Finally, we made it across the mountains and into Nepal, where we were instantly detained by the Nepali police. We spent some time in a jail, and didn't know what would happen next. Fortunately for us, Nepal is home to lots of Tibetan refugees, and although they didn't allow resettlement there, they allowed us to pass through the country to reach India rather than hand us back to the Chinese.

By this stage of the journey, all I had was a few yuan and an empty bag. Finally, I was taken from the Nepali jail by the Tibetan Reception Centre, which organized my transfer to India. There were two people, a brother and a sister, who helped me a lot. They were kind to me, and even now I feel grateful to them even though I still don't know their names.

When I left Tibet, I had biscuits and drinks, but I made the two-day journey from Nepal to India without a single meal. I had 800 yuan on me when I left. Some of the money was lost on the way and some was given to the leader for our journey. In India, I was sent to Dharamsala, home of our exiled leader, His Holiness the Dalai Lama. I had never been to school before, but in India, I was sent to a Tibetan Children Village School, where I received the education my mother had always hoped I would get.

Once I had joined the school, I lived there from 1997 to 2008 without any vacations because I had nobody to care for me outside.

Now, 18 years later, I live in Bengaluru, working as a chef. I regularly travel back to Dharamsala for religious teachings from the Dalai Lama. I am planning on leaving my job as a chef to pursue further education. I want to learn Chinese, improve my English and Tibetan, and study Buddhist philosophy.

I still think fondly of Tibet, with the innocent memories of childhood, but I don't think I will ever be able to return. I would like to, and I tried to last year, but I think it is not possible just yet. If I were to return now, I'd have to report to the local Chinese police every week, or there would be an enquiry. Returning would make me a criminal.

I still call my mother sometimes, but it's quite difficult to connect. It's also risky for her to be talking to me.

To me, it is really important that the world learns and hears about the plight of the Tibetan people. My story is really just a drop in the ocean. I have heard stories of some Tibetans who were caught more than four times by the Chinese government, but still they struggle to run away to India.

I cannot speak too much about what is happening over there these days as it has been 18 years since I left. But army officials are spread through all corners of every city. Even around monasteries, people are carrying guns. This is ridiculous and disrespectful of their prayers for a peaceful and healthy world. Nowadays, in Tibet, the majority of the people are Chinese. The environment is suffering as there is intense coal mining, major defor-estation, and loss of wildlife. There are more factories, more pollution, and more people, but fewer farmers. The nomadic people are in a critical posi-tion because they used to trade butter and cheese for rice, wheat, and grain with the farmers, who are slowly disappearing.

I am just one example; there are many other Tibetans in exile with much more serious problems and in much worse situations. To be given this opportunity to tell my story, I would like to thank many people. I am very grateful to the Indian government for their democracy. More than that, they care for us like we are their own citizens, their brothers and sisters. I also want to thank His Holiness the 14th Dalai Lama. He is everything to our Tibetan community. We Tibetans have been spread across the world as refugees, but thanks to His Holiness's effort and greatness, there is concern in the world for us. We have a beautiful Tibetan democratic government in exile, thanks to him; he has held us all together. There are a thousand reasons we are thankful to His Holiness the Dalai Lama, but for now I will leave it here.

We are not hoping for much, but we dream of achieving freedom, peace, and a protected and thriving environment.

—As told to Melanie Groves

UKRAINE

'The heart of Europe is in Ukraine.'

Victor Yushchenko

As of 2016, more than 1.65 million people had been displaced in Ukraine. Ukraine came to experience the phenomenon of forced migration since 2014 and a lot of Ukrainians applied for asylum in other countries. The applications for asylum were mostly directed towards Russia and the European Union (EU) countries.

Public protests demanding closer ties with the EU and the resignation of President Viktor Yanukovych began in late 2013, leading to widespread civil unrest and, ultimately, the revolution of 2014.

Russia, prompted by counter-revolutionary sentiment in the Crimean Peninsula, staged a military intervention and subsequently annexed the region in a move largely condemned by the international community. Fighting between government forces and pro-Russian separatists has continued despite domestic and international efforts to de-escalate the crisis.

I Have Nothing to Go Back To

It was a Sunday, in the spring of 2014. I don't remember the exact date, but the war in Donbass had already started. My home town, Horlivka, north of Donetsk city, was not spared. We had nothing left to eat at home, so my mother had to go out to buy something. I never saw her again. There was shelling in the town that day.

My name is Evgheni and I am 17 years old. My mother and I were living in an apartment on the outskirts of Horlivka, near the lakes. Our family was not rich, but we managed. We had all we needed: food on the table, clothes, some money. I was in high school. But that was all before the war. After the Euromaidan revolution, everything changed. The values of the euro and the dollar went up, so the money my mother was making became lesser and, hence, wasn't sufficient. The stores became more and more expensive and war added to the equation. There was not much left to buy anyway. Life turned hard.

In April 2014, the separatists came to my home town. They hoisted the Russian flag on top of the police station and started confiscating the houses and cars of the wealthy classes. I did not know many of them, the town being quite big as it is. And they did not look like Ukrainians; they had a Caucasian resemblance. Then the Ukrainian army came and the war started in Horlivka.

I remember people awaiting their arrival, but I am not aware when exactly it happened. I had other things on my mind back then. I was into IT and I did not think the situation was too serious. But then, homes started being hit by the shelling. The separatists would blame it on the Ukrainian army, but the army did not bomb the houses, only the streets. I would crawl on the floor, hide under a chair, or any place I could find, and just wait for it to be over. It wasn't safe anywhere, not outside certainly, but not even in your own home.

One day, our apartment was hit. The Grad missile entered through the window. Thank God none of us was home. I could not believe my eyes when I arrived: everything was destroyed. And I was all alone; my mother was gone. We both loved each other very much; I can't imagine her leaving me behind. I feared something definitely serious would have happened to her. And I fear the worst. Two days after she did not return, I started looking for her. At first, I thought she had sought refuge in a neighbour's house. But she was not there. I started calling some relatives in the other part of the town. But they did not pick up. I ran through the town for days looking for her. But she was nowhere to be found. At night, I would have to stop my search because of the intense fighting.

I lived alone for over a year, in the basement of our apartment building. For half a year, I lived on boiled wheat alone. There was a neighbour who helped me though. She would bring me some soup and bread once in a while.

In the last couple of weeks, the separatists started visiting us and bringing food to me and some friends that I shared the basement with. One of them was a neighbour, fighting for the Donetsk People's Republic. He tried to convince me to join them, said they need more soldiers. 'We have enough weapons,' he said, 'but we need more men to fight.' I did not want to. One day I received a message on my mobile phone saying, 'If you are not with us, you will die'.

I left Horlivka that same day. I packed what little I had—a pair of trousers, a vest, two pairs of socks, and my phone—and I ran. I borrowed 300 euros from the neighbour who used to bring me food, hoping that some day I would be able to repay her.

I passed the separatist check point on foot; nobody had been willing to help me. I almost got caught. I ran through the forest, creeping on my belly through the fields. I was afraid the soldiers at the Ukrainian army check point would think I was a separatist, so I hid in a car among a man's merchandise.

The first night I slept between two corpses. The field was full of bodies that seemed to have been brought there and left to rot. It was August; the air was hot and thick with the smell of the dead. I thought if someone saw me, they would think I was dead. I was so afraid I would get caught; there was nothing in my mind except that I had to run.

I reached Krasnoarmeysk on foot. There, a man took me in his car up to Dnipropetrovsk. After that, I stopped a truck. I saw it coming in the distance and just stepped in the middle of the road. The driver said I was nuts. He was going to Austria, so I offered to pay him to take me across the borders, somewhere in Europe, more to the west. I was scared to stay in Ukraine, I worried they would find me. And who knew what would happen next in my country?

I crossed two borders hidden in boxes in the back of the truck—the one with the Republic of Moldova and the other into Romania. Somehow, I was lucky and no one discovered me. The 100 euros I paid the truck driver got me up to Suceava, in Romania. There, he told me that I was on my own from that point onward. I wanted to go further west, so I took a night coach from Suceava to Cluj-Napoca. I fell asleep. When I woke up, people on the coach told me I must have had a very bad dream, as I was shaking and trembling in my sleep. If only they knew …

From Cluj-Napoca, I took the train westwards to Oradea and then tried to cross the border with Hungary. I knew Romania was in the EU, but I made the mistake to believe it is also part of the Schengen Area, so I decided to cross the border on foot. That's when I got caught.

My grandmother was Romanian. She came to Ukraine during the Soviet era and married my grandfather, a Ukrainian national. My mother was born in Horlivka, but she was taught Romanian, and she had taught me the language as well. I started speaking in Romanian with the border police and they believed I was from the Republic of Moldova. I had left home in a hurry, and hadn't taken any documents; half of them had been burnt in the explosion anyway. I told the police I was from the Donetsk region, so they sent a request to Ukraine. But there, it does not work like in Romania or other European countries; there, each region has its own databases. The police did not get any reply from Donetsk. I spent two days in the centre for asylum seekers. After that, I was transferred to a shelter run by an NGO in Timișoara.

I want to learn how to live here, in Romania. I want to go to college here and become an electrical engineer. I have nothing to go back to in Ukraine. My mother is gone, my house is gone. Most of my friends are gone: some dead, some ran away, and others are fighting for the separatists.

I miss my mother. I looked for her each day for over a week. I could not find her anywhere. I don't have much hope left, but now that I am safe, I will try to search for her again. I will call the police or anyone who might help me.

People say that experiences make you unique. So yes, I am unique, but at what cost? I start shaking with fear even if I just recall everything that I have been through. Dead men, dead women, dead children. Dead soldiers. All dead. I don't wish what I have witnessed in my lifetime upon anyone. And I am afraid it won't go away anytime soon.

My name is Evgheni and I will be 18 years old in March 2016.

Evgheni is not his real name. He chose not to divulge his identity, due to concerns related to the asylum procedure.

YEMEN

'Faith is the cure that heals all troubles.
Without faith, there is no hope and no love.
Faith comes before hope, and before love.'

Paul Torday, *Salmon Fishing in the Yemen*

By August 2015, with the outbreak of civil war in January and major foreign intervention, the number of internally displaced Yemenis alone is thought to have risen to about 1.5 million, about 6 per cent of the population. The number is five times what it was in December 2014. At the end of 2016, the figure for IDPs due to conflict and violence stood at more than 1.97 million.

A large population of Yemenis is severely food-insecure, which means that any further problem, even a small one, could push them to the brink of starvation. Only half the Yemeni population has access to potable water. The country's hospitals have closed in droves and the physicians and nurses have fled, so millions have been left without medical care.

Thousands are leaving every week, taking passage in cargo ships across the Red Sea to Djibouti and Somalia in the Horn of Africa, and some are making their way north to places like Egypt.

Because Yemen is so much farther from Europe, its tragedy has received less press attention than Syria's, but its wars could be even more disruptive.

A Future Full of Question Marks

The contrast in their demeanour could not be more stark. One full of fire and gripe against her forced homelessness, the other a traditionalist to the core who speaks in a soft, measured tone in the face of an extreme existential challenge. I met both women at a refugee services agency in Addis Ababa that had begun the registration process for the latest batch of refugees from Yemen. These women, having escaped the war in Yemen, are picking up the pieces of their broken lives, their middle-class dreams of peace and normality shattered to bits by a war that will soon rival Syria in the scale of devastation and the humanitarian disaster facing the country. Waad bemoans the loss of her callow childhood and the abrupt coming of age in exile. Lina, mother of a boy, misses things that she was used to: 'her own house, car, her friends, her country, and her old city Sana'a, its traditions and its heritage, the sea back home, and, oh yes, the food'.

Ever since the revolution started in Yemen almost five years ago, my mother has been a refugee in the Ethiopian capital, Addis Ababa. When our neighbourhoods of Ali Mohsin and Hamid al Hamar in Sanaa became the scene of constant fighting, I advised my mother, a divorcée and a house-wife, to leave the country along with my son while I would stay back to support the family. Samir, my older brother who lived with our mother, also left. I had been to Addis before as a tourist. A friend of mine had moved here in good times and I would visit her every other year.

The hardest part about being a refugee is that one misses things that one is used to—your own house, car, your friends, your country and city, its traditions and heritage, the sea back home, and, oh yes, the food. You leave when things lose all meaning and life leaves you with no options. Overnight, all these things are snatched away. I am the same person who used to travel, float like a butterfly between Sana'a and Taiz, and all the way to Aden when the sea beckoned. Now I live in a one–room tenement in a downcast neighbourhood on the outskirts of Addis because that's the rent that I can afford nowadays. The past has simply been blasted away.

I had a decent childhood, populated with happy memories and lots of cousins with whom I spent all my time playing. The happier memories are of times spent with my maternal grandparents. They were generous with their time and love.

My mother has always been a kind-hearted, good woman, but a weak person. She suffered a great deal at my father's hands. He mistreated her for years and she bore it without complaining. He deprived her all the time, and would ask her to manage her expenses by herself. Despite being the wife of a well-to-do man, she went out to work at a beauty salon. She wanted her children to never miss out on a good life and did all that was in her power to make it possible.

As a successful timber merchant, my father must have been a rich man. But he blew it all away on his own indulgences, including heavy drinking and womanizing. I still remember one time when he went to Addis for a visit and never once called our mother. After waiting patiently for his call for days, she finally called the hotel where he was staying. The lady receptionist rather indulgently told her not to be too worried about her husband as he was being looked after well by a beautiful woman.

Now in the sunset of his life, my father is a changed man: calm, almost meditative, and very friendly. My mother has no feelings for him. Nor do I. I wish he was like this when we were growing up.

I had an arranged marriage with a man who used to work in the DHL courier company. His mother made all the decisions in the house and never quite took a shine to me. She and the rest of the family treated me as a maid, expecting me to take charge of the household chores. My time was spent cleaning and dusting the whole house, including the separate living quarters of my parents-in-law, and cooking for my family. I was expected to entertain and feed my husband's friends who used to be in the house frequently for their drinking parties, musical soirées, and for chewing qat, an age-old social custom among men in Yemen of feasting on a local herb that worked as a stimulant.

I was all of 20 when I got married. My son Ahmed was born when I was 21. I left my husband when my son was not even a year old. My marriage with this man that I did not know before and had little in common with never quite took off. We used to fight all the time. He was too callous and indifferent towards my needs from him as a person.

The final straw came in the form of an ugly argument. One night, I asked him to bring milk for our son. He showed up late, as always, without even bringing the milk. Deeply upset, I walked out of the house with my son and went to my uncle's place who used to stay close to my in-laws' house. I stayed the night at my uncle's house and when I went back the next morning, my mother-in-law got into an ugly spat with me. She was so enraged by my act of defiance in leaving my husband's house all alone in the dead of the night—something that is not considered appropriate—that she got physical. She said the family honour had been sullied by my act. I couldn't take it any more and decided to leave.

I filed for divorce soon after but it took a good nine months to complete the process. Come to think of it, my parents stayed together much longer, but that was mainly because my mother was weak and indecisive. I have seen my mother suffer in silence and make her marriage work, come what may, simply to give her children the opportunity to be loved by both their parents.

After my divorce, I was able to feel free again. Except for the occasional stress of having to deal with a difficult uncle, my mother's brother, who had decided to be rude to me and lost no opportunity to remind me that as a divorcée I was expected to be a clean and chaste woman, I was able to regain my strength. The court decided that I would have the custody of Ahmed while my husband was allowed to meet his son on Thursdays and Sundays. He hardly ever came to visit, but I was too glad to be free of the manacles of a loveless marriage and to be out of the house that treated me as a maid. No more.

At work though, it wasn't all hunky-dory. It all started with one gentleman who asked me out for a date. I couldn't have agreed, not least, because by this time I was already seeing a nice French guy who happened to be living in Sana'a and working in the oil industry. While handling an administrative function in the company, I found massive corruption in the form of fake invoices that the managers expected to be approved and live off as perks. I brought this to the attention of the highest authorities. They hated my guts and my attitude and decided to come together to make life difficult for me at the workplace.

Threats were handed out and security men were put on my trail. They used to follow me everywhere and keep the managers informed of my movements. It all got extremely suffocating. This coincided with the period when the Saudis decided to intervene to fix the political situation in Yemen through strong military action. Bombs rained day and night on Sana'a and there was not a place in the whole city that was not shattered and devastated. As someone who had grown in the city, it was too painful to watch it turn to rubble.

The incessant violence, coupled with the insistent harassment at the hands of my superiors in office, finally forced me to take the decision to move out of the country. By this time, my French friend, who had been a source of great support and unlimited joy for me, had left the country, as had most, if not all, the internationals living in Yemen, thanks to the advisories issued by almost every Western capital to its citizens.

I never imagined my life would come to this. That I would become a refugee one day, live a hand-to-mouth existence, and be staring at a future full of question marks, having no idea how and where my son would grow up. Given the grave security situation in Sana'a, my company allowed me to leave the city temporarily, and they continue to pay me almost two-thirds of my salary. With the economy now completely tanked back home, it is only a matter of time before my company will stop extending the perks of paying me even a part of the salary that they currently do. I shudder to think how I will support my current lifestyle and the needs of my son and my ageing mother.

I want to go out there and work. Qatar would be fine to live if I found work there. Or for that matter any Gulf state. All I want now is to be able to live well, something that I have been used to for years. And to be able to afford a good school for my son.

No Time or Will to Be of
Help to Others

For as long as I can remember, my father hardly lived with us. For the most part, he lived in his sister's house. There was a time when he did not visit us for three years in a row. It was in the summer of 2012, when my sister, Jamila, and I were visiting my aunt in Ethiopia during our holidays, that my mother finally filed for divorce. We had planned to spend three months there, but officials from the Yemeni embassy summoned us and asked us to return home where the court wanted to seek our consent on parental custody. We rushed back home. In the court, all three of us—my sister, my younger brother, and I—chose to stay with our mother.

Though I may look completely Yemeni, I have some Ethiopian blood in me, thanks to my maternal grandmother, who is half-Ethiopian. I picked up Amharic, the local Ethiopian language, at an early age from my mother. As a refugee in Ethiopia, it does make life just a bit easier as I can speak to anyone and everyone here with ease.

But Sana'a is where most of my life was lived even as we used to visit our native home in the village of Taiz for vacations. My father, like so many men of his generation in Yemen, suffered from all kinds of addictions—chewing qat, drinking, drugs. All his nights were spent in personal recreations, away from his family. He always woke up late and went to work late.

He was constantly in and out of jobs as no employer liked his wayward lifestyle and lack of punctuality and discipline when it came to performing his official duties. I must have been 12 or 13 when I started recognizing his faults. I remember feeling unhappy and crying about our family life because of my father's strange and selfish lifestyle.

Our home used to be in Fejatan, a mountainous area just outside Sana'a. It was a sparse little rented apartment, but snug and cozy with the love that we shared with our mother. It was well known in our neighbourhood that before demitting office, the former president, Abdullah Saleh, had dug up whole mountains in Fejatan where he had hidden away a massive cache of weapons and explosives. We lived right at the base of these hills within a 2-km radius. President Saleh, before he sought exile in Saudi Arabia, decided to destroy the weapons lest they fell into enemy hands. Before we knew it, he had launched an air campaign on the mountainside to achieve this objective.

The Saudi aerial action in Sana'a started during the night of 25 May 2015. For days and nights without end, I remember we used to squirm in fear of bombs flying overhead and hoping that the bombs do not get dropped off target and take our house. It must have been a massive cache of ammunition that the former president had hidden away for it took his forces days and weeks together to explode it all. Countless perished in their sleep.

Within days, the bombings became more indiscriminate, as schools, homes, and hospitals were hit. Everything around us was turning into rubble. The Houthis started using citizens as weapons of war as a siege was laid to keep food aid and other essential items out of reach for those of us living in the mountain areas. No one was able to leave their homes.

As it is, we were hearing about massive fuel shortages and how public transportation in the form of buses and taxis was coming to a grinding halt.

Our place was located not even 400 metres from the base of the mountains which were now at the centre of Saleh's action. Fear engulfed the entire neighbourhood and we could see a steady flight of people wanting to move out to safer locations.

Our hearts were filled with fright and terror by the high-decibel sound of the bombs, but we carried on living in our home. We survived the bombings for three months, and when we could not take it any longer, we decided to move out to the relative safety of our uncle's home some 6 km away in the Asbahi area. My uncle and his wife were kind and generous and took us in with grace and without fuss. For the next three months, we lived out of our boxes and bags. When there was a temporary let-up in the bombings, we would move back to our own home, and when it got more intense again, we would run to our uncle's place.

On 18 June, the Ethiopian government invited Yemenis of Ethiopian descent or with any filial Ethiopian connections to live temporarily in Ethiopia. My mother's connection entitled us to benefit from this offer. We were among the last ones to avail of this invitation and be registered as refugees in Ethiopia.

We arrived in Addis Ababa on the second day of the holy month of Ramadan. Within just two days of our arrival, my loving aunt Maimuna, who had arrived just two days before us, took seriously ill. She had been suffering from several health complications back in Yemen and had previously even travelled as far as Bangkok and Cairo for treatment. But we all felt the non-stop and high-decibel bombing in areas close to her house in Sana'a that eventually led her to abandon her house was the last straw that broke her already battered will to fight for her own survival. She was ill-prepared to live the vagrant life of a refugee and got too affected psychologically by the thought of being homeless. Finally, she succumbed to her illness on the 26th day of Ramadan.

Upon arrival in Addis, we spent the first month with another aunt who had been living there for years. Since this was the month of Ramadan, we decided to take it easy and start looking for an apartment to rent in due course. But things move quickly in life. It is already several months now since we have been living on our own, as refugees in an alien land. The Ethiopian Agency for Refugee Rehabilitation with the support of the UN refugee agency has started extending to us meagre financial assistance. We also have of late been benefitting from the rehabilitation services extended by the JRS. Jamila goes twice a week to the JRS to participate in English language and computer classes. Back home, I wasted two years because of the conflict that made it impossible to go to school.

Now in a safe place, I have resumed my preparations for writing my Grade 12 exam.

Even though I can speak Amharic, I am not so good at reading and writing in the language. All my life up to this stage, my studies were all in Arabic, but now, if I have to pursue higher studies as a refugee, I need to train myself quickly to read and write in the national language of Ethiopia. It is a daunting thought.

Survival as a refugee is too expensive. Life in Sana'a was affordable and our mother had a stable if limited income of 6,000 Yemeni riyals (or USD 300). With that money, we had a decent, though by no means luxurious, life. But here in exile, we cannot afford the most basic of services. House rent and food expenses alone wipe away almost all of our meagre allowance of USD 140 or 3,500 Ethiopian birr that we get for the whole family. The apartment that we have rented almost 20 km on the outskirts of Addis is a cubbyhole, with just a room and a bathroom, not even a proper kitchen. In Sana'a, we had a room for each of us, two restrooms, and a large verandah overlooking the majestic mountains. That view was priceless. All that has changed.

There was a time when I dreamt of becoming an engineer. I thought I had it in me to be a technically qualified professional. To some extent, it was the pride of inheritance, as my father was known to be of a technically accomplished mind. But I know it will never be the same again. I know I can never go back to the Yemen in which I was born and raised. That home, that life does not exist. I have to move on, find a life in other countries, and sing the music of life in harmony with my adopted home.

At this stage, my only dream is to complete my studies and be of some tangible help to my family, to have a good income and a stable life, be able to afford house rent, and one day, Insha'Allah, even buy a car. I am already considering a few options for part-time paid work: tailoring women's clothes, cooking food for small restaurants, marketing my services to NGOs as an Amaharic–Arabic translator. And I am still eager to learn English. Not knowing the language well is a big blindspot that I want to overcome, because English opens doors for work everywhere. So many people speak English.

Refugees are disallowed by law to seek employment in Ethiopia. If only the government allowed it, I would take a job immediately and take on a bit of the financial burden on behalf of my family. I thank Allah that in these months as refugees, we have not had a major illness in the family even though each of us has had skin rashes, cold, and flu by turns. In our dire conditions these days, we can hardly afford an illness. There is a UN-run health facility in Addis that we visit from time to time for treatment of minor problems.

The Christians and Muslims live far apart from each other and do not seem to socialize much. From what I have seen of Ethiopian society, they all seem kind and cohesive and imbued with a deep faith in God. Still, I find that people do not have much sympathy for refugees. It may have to do with the fact that most Ethiopians are struggling to make ends meet. We were used to being shown respect even by strangers. Out here, I find that our dignity as individuals has nearly collapsed. In buses, we are pushed around and sometimes even looked at with hate and talked to as if we deserve no respect.

I do not approve of the way Ethiopian girls dress. Wearing short and revealing dresses is forbidden in Islam. This kind of dressing is not good for leading a moral life. But it is their life and I should learn to accept the society here as it is. To tell you the truth, I am not into relationships at all. Never have been. I have learnt a bitter lesson from the experiences of my mother. It is not that I hate men. But I love myself more and will choose a job over a man any time and every time. Jamila is different. She is more impressionable and spontaneous and could fall into a relationship any time.

In these past months as a refugee, I have had the opportunity to observe my Yemeni society very closely. I see they have become aloof from each other. A strange kind of narrow, fragmented self-interest seems to have set in amongst us. We seem to have become incapable of reaching out to our less fortunate brothers and sisters. Each one of us seems to be withdrawing deeper and deeper into his or her own world of daily miseries and struggles, with no time or will to be of any help to others who might need it.

Afterword

More humans are on the run today than at any time in recorded history. Conflicts rank among the foremost man-made causes for human displacement. The UNHCR reported in 2016 that an unprecedented 65 million people were displaced around the world due to war and persecution. Aid and refugee organizations are stretched beyond limits in coping with the sheer scale of human displacement.

The uptick in displacement is partly attributed to over seven years of brutal war in Syria. Aid agencies estimate that nearly half of the Syrian population has lost its home, some on multiple occasions, during the last seven years of the conflict. The actual numbers could arguably be higher, as gathering definitive data in the war-ravaged country has been a massive challenge. The governorates of Ar-Raqqa and Deir Ez-Zor in the north-east of the country have been particularly difficult to access given the presence of ISIS.

While the media spotlight has been on Europe's challenge of managing more than 1 million refugees—a vast majority from Syria, Iraq, Afghanistan, Somalia, and Eritrea—and migrants who arrived via the Mediterranean, it is often forgotten that the vast majority of the world's refugees were in developing countries in the global south. In all, 86 per cent of the refugees under the UNHCR's mandate in 2015 were in low- and middle-income countries close to situations of conflict. Ethiopia is a prime example of a third-world country accounting for a vast majority of refugees from South Sudan, Eritrea, Yemen, and the Democratic Republic of Congo (DRC). In Syria, close to 5 million have fled to neighbouring countries like Turkey, Lebanon, Jordan, Egypt, and even to northern Iraq; some 7 million are displaced within the country. Worldwide, Turkey is the biggest host country, with 2.5 million refugees. With nearly one refugee for every five citizens, Lebanon hosts more refugees compared to its population than any other country.

Somalia and Afghanistan are now well into their third and fourth decade of conflicts respectively. These conflicts have taken an untold toll of human suffering and caused massive outflows of people into neighbouring countries. Add to this the dramatic rise of unresolved conflicts in countries such as Yemen, Iraq, South Sudan, Ukraine, and the Central African Republic (CAR), to name but a handful, that have seen the bloodiest conflicts in recent times and caused homelessness at a scale rarely seen in recorded history.

Among the world's 21 million refugees, children under the age of 18 made up an astonishing 51 per cent of the world's refugees in 2015, according to the UNHCR data published in its flagship Global Trends report. Many were separated from their parents or travelling alone.

The total headcount of IDPs worldwide as a result of conflict and violence stood at just under 41 million people, almost double the total number of refugees. While the plight of the world's 19.5 million refugees is now firmly on the political and media agenda because of the European refugee crisis, its IDP population is often forgotten.

Five of the 10 countries with the highest number of conflict-driven IDPs—Colombia, DRC, Iraq, Sudan, and, since independence in 2011, South Sudan—have appeared in the IDMC's list every year since 2003.

Call them IDPs, refugees, asylum seekers, stateless persons or whatever, it is a global crisis of epic proportions. Despite the differences in legal status and of entitlement to aid from the international humanitarian community, the causes of displacement and the experience of being displaced are often similar for both IDPs and refugees. Much like refugees, IDPs often feel like strangers in their place of refuge.

Data from the Norwegian Refugee Council's IDMC shows that in 2015 alone, violence displaced 8.6 million more people last year—24,000 each day on average—making it a record year for conflict-driven displacement. There are also 10 million stateless people who have been denied a nationality and access to basic rights such as education, healthcare, employment, and freedom of movement.

Conflicts in the Middle East and North Africa continue to take an unprecedented toll. Yemen, Syria, and Iraq today account for over half of the global total of conflict-induced displacement. Aside from the Middle East, Ukraine, Nigeria, DRC, Afghanistan, Colombia, CAR, and South Sudan had the highest numbers of new IDPs.

More than one country in Latin America is convulsed by prolonged insurgency, and added to that is the generalized criminal violence associated with drug trafficking and gang activity that has displaced at least 1 million people in Mexico, El Salvador, Guatemala, and Honduras.

Those running to save themselves from being caught in conflicts take to the sea and land with equal desperation. At sea, a frightening number of refugees and migrants are dying each year. On land, people fleeing war are finding their way blocked by closed borders. Nearly half a million people fleeing war, persecution, and extreme poverty reached Europe in 2016. The UN-affiliated International Organization for Migration reported that at least 7,500 people died in 2016 while crossing the Mediterranean as they tried to reach Europe. The number of fatalities witnessed a 34 per cent jump over 2015. Many shipwrecks occurred on the route between Libya and the Italian island of Sicily. The central Mediterranean route linking the Sahara region to southern Europe still operates at full capacity despite European efforts to stem the flow.

'Life as a refugee is dehumanizing. I cannot take the daily slurs,' Odai, a Syrian refugee that I met in Izmir in Turkey told me. Twice, Odai has moved within Turkey alone after escaping the war in Aleppo. 'I want to go back and die in my homeland. But I know my children will never let me take them back. It's been a year since we left and they still get nightmares thinking of the bombs that rained in our neighbourhoods.'

Human displacement caused by an ever-increasing frequency of natural disasters such as droughts, floods, cyclones, and earthquakes is many times higher. Natural disasters forced over 19 million people in 113 countries out of their homes—more than twice the number made homeless by conflict. Over the past eight years, a staggering 203 million people have been displaced due to disasters. Case studies point to hundreds of thousands of disaster-affected people living in protracted displacement, some for up to dozens of years, without any resolution in sight. But that is a different story all together.

The thousands of men, women, and children streaming through the borders of Europe have finally drawn the world's attention to a historic crisis. For the first time in its history, Europe finds an influx of humanity from outside the continent knocking at its doors for asylum.

A UNICEF report, 'A Deadly Journey for Children: The Central Mediterranean Migrant Route', provides an in-depth look at the extreme risks facing refugee and migrant children as they make the perilous journey from sub-Saharan Africa into Libya and across the sea to Italy. Three quarters of the refugee and migrant children interviewed as part of a survey said they had experienced violence, harassment, or aggression at the hands of adults at some point over the course of their journey, while nearly half of the women and children interviewed reported sexual abuse during migration—often multiple times and in multiple locations.

The Central Mediterranean Route has become a massive people-smuggling operation, which has grown out of control for the lack of safe and alternative migration systems. It exploits porous and corrupt border security, the sparse Saharan terrain, and the vacuum created by the Libyan conflict.

The European response to this refugee crisis has lacked coherence, even bordering on the shambolic. Germany is among the few countries that have been willing to welcome a substantial number of refugees and sought a common European strategy to deal with the crisis. Other nations have locked down their borders, crammed refugees into transit camps. Some have expressed open reluctance to taking in Muslims, by far the largest religious group of asylum seekers.

Just when Europeans thought that widespread economic stagnation and the Greek debt crisis were their biggest problems, came the refugee influx, predominantly from the conflict-affected Muslim world. To be fair, Europe has faced large refugee movements before, the Bosnia and Kosovo conflicts of the 1990s for instance. However, this is the first time in its history that Europe has faced a mass influx of refugees from outside the region.

The defeat of Nazi Germany and its allies led to the displacement of an estimated 25 million people. Between 6 and 7 million ethnic Germans were expelled from eastern Europe and the territory annexed from the German Reich between 1944 and 1946. The overwhelming majority of them settled in what became West Germany.

Compare these figures with the fewer than 70,000 refugees who arrived in the United States in 2013. The US is still contending with a problem one-eighth the size of Germany's—and with a total population four times larger. Syrians are only one among many nationalities claiming asylum in Europe. In the first half of this year, tens of thousands of Afghans and Eritreans also made the hazardous journey to Europe, as did thousands of Nigerians, Pakistanis, Somalis, Sudanese, and Iraqis. There are many more where they came from.

Our inability to learn from history condemns us to repeat mistakes. Many credit Europe for having been the architects of the modern international legal instruments for protection of people fleeing war, persecution, and worse. The 1951 Refugee Convention is believed to have been triggered by the desire of the European states to restore fundamental rights to the holocaust survivors. There are other more recent historical lessons that are important today. The Vietnamese refugee crisis of 1975 is another example. Millions of Vietnamese refugees fled by boats to South East Asian states. Many drowned as boats were pushed back. But in both 1979 and 1989, international agreements were made such that some 1.8 million people were resettled around the world. The key was international cooperation, recognizing that refugee protection is a shared, global responsibility.

Another lesson that is lost on the world is the costs of protracted displacement. Over half the world's refugees have been in exile for at least five years, many in closed refugee camps where they do not have the right to work or move freely. Many end up as cannon fodder and willing recruits for radical ideologies—a colossal waste of human lives with all its attendant consequences. With a fairer and more humane approach and a mix of enabling policies, the refugees could be trained in vocational skills, their talents deployed for social and economic development.

The scale of the refugee challenge to Europe calls for a clear-headed approach that is based on recognizing the capacities rather than just the vulnerabilities of refugees. Uganda, another developing country in Africa that is hemmed in by the refugee crisis, is showing the way. The country has adopted a Self-Reliance Strategy that gives refugees the right to work and significant freedom of movement. These kinds of policies can lead to better outcomes for refugees and host communities.

Greece and Italy face the physical crush of arrivals, while Germany, Sweden, and Britain are where most migrants want to go. And in-between are nearly two dozen countries that do not see migration as their problem. Europe's system for accepting migrants doesn't work. This migration crisis has given a high-profile platform to xenophobia. It has led Hungary, where numbers of migrants entering have dramatically spiked, to start building a wall. The Slovakian government said it will accept refugees from Syria but only Christian ones, not Muslims.

In the heated discussion about Europe's migration crisis, which can bleed into the wider debate over security and terrorism, it's easy to forget the most important lesson of all. Each migrant is a person, with families back home and a lifetime of aspiration and regret behind him or her.

I captured the human element by following the story of a Syrian refugee in Vienna. Working in a small hotel by night and continuing his undergrad school by day, he still feels anxious for the safety and security of his mother and father who he left behind in Aleppo.

During the course of my travels across countries that bore the brunt of the refugee influx, I came face to face with human smuggling. Izmir, Turkey's third-largest city, was ground zero for shady smugglers who charged a cool USD 1,000 per person for helping the refugees cross the roughly 20-km-long stretch across the Aegean Sea into Greece.

Refugees find smugglers on social media, run a basic check by asking others who might have used their services, and prepare themselves to take the plunge. The smuggler arranges the dinghies, leads the journey, and jumps the boat before the border patrols on the Greek side can apprehend them.

Countries like Slovenia, Croatia, Macedonia, and Serbia have closed their borders to refugees who, for the most part, transit through these countries before dropping anchor in some of the more economically stable countries in western Europe. The new closures are part of an EU deal with Turkey. The deal requires Turkey to repatriate migrants who land in Greece. In a bizarre quid pro quo, Europe will accept one asylum seeker from Turkey for each refugee returned. Other than giving EU countries breathing space and allowing them to be selective about whom they accept within their borders, it is hard to see how this exchange will give Europe much relief.

But this does not solve the problem of those who have already arrived. Estimates place the number of asylum seekers who entered Europe in 2015 alone at 1.8 million. Fewer than 3,00,000 have been granted asylum. The fate of the rest hangs in the balance. Greece, already on its knees because of its debt crisis, faces a major chunk of the refugee problem. As many as 2,00,000 refugees may be in the country with 2,000–3,000 more arriving each day. These desperate people will certainly resist being returned to Turkey. Official closures notwithstanding, some of those in Greece will try to cross land borders, none of which can be completely secured. Anticipating trouble, Hungary has already beefed up its border police. Other asylum seekers will find other, safer sea routes to reach places like Italy. One can expect to hear more shipwrecks of the type that killed 800 asylum seekers in April 2015.

Despite the ripples that can be seen in Europe and North America, the civil and political conflicts that have caused so many millions to run for cover and safety in faraway lands don't seem to be anywhere near ending. Conflicts ride on the back of divisions and schisms of religion and politics that have been with us for decades. There is hardly any sign that confronting the causes and seeking consensus and reconciliation is on the minds of either the parties to the conflicts or indeed the whole gaggle of professional do-gooders that have thrived on the rather genteel talk of peace-making. The US has just announced an astronomical increase in its military spending, signalling its resolve to up its game against the terror networks, all with the stated objective of keeping America safe. Once again, the salt of the earth will bear the brunt of the increasingly violent methods that are sought to be deployed to resolve rather elemental questions of fair play and justice in the world. Migration out of conflict zones will escalate to another level. And, who knows, we might be looking at the 100-million displaced mark sooner than we can imagine.

The one lesson that the US can feasibly draw from Europe's refugee crisis is that no matter how high the border walls, people will find ways of getting into the land of hope, freedom, and opportunity. For one, there is the thousand-mile-long coastline that offers a way into the country. The threats and blandishments to deport 10 million and more undocumented immigrants, aside from militating against the very values that are at the heart of this immigrant nation, will only serve to give rise to a gargantuan new bureaucracy and a hyper-police state hitherto unseen in its history.

One of the first things Donald Trump did on assuming office was pass an executive order—protecting the nation from foreign terrorist entry into the United States—imposing a 90-day travel ban, with some exceptions, on the citizens of seven predominately Muslim countries: Iraq, Syria, Iran, Sudan, Libya, Somalia, and Yemen. The order had also suspended the US Refugee Admissions Program for 120 days. In addition, it indefinitely prohibited Syrian refugees from entering the US.

Legal challenges to the executive order were underway a day after Trump signed it. The American Civil Liberties Union lawyers won a temporary stay in federal court in Brooklyn, New York, allowing those with valid visas and refugee approvals who had arrived to the US or were en route to remain in the country. Federal judges in four other states—California, Virginia, Massachusetts, and Washington—followed with orders that temporarily stayed parts of the executive order.

The point of the order was to keep would-be foreign terrorists out of the country. That raises the question of how many foreign-born people have committed such crimes in the US to begin with. Trump's executive order directed the secretary of homeland security and the US attorney general to find out.

Others, though, had already compiled some of that information. One of them, Alex Nowrasteh, an immigration policy analyst at the Cato Institute, produced a 28-page report in 2016 called 'Terrorism and Immigration'. Nowrasteh's report identified 154 foreign-born people who were convicted of carrying out or attempting to carry out a terrorist attack in the US over a 40-year period, from 1975 to 2015, most of them on or after 11 September 2001. Forty of the 154 were responsible for 3,024 deaths; 114 of them were not responsible for any deaths.

Only 17 of the 154 foreign-born terrorists were from the seven countries covered by the Trump administration's temporary travel ban. But none of the 17 was responsible for any deaths—even though the seven countries combined represented almost 40 per cent of all refugees accepted into the US in the last 10 years.

As of 31 January 2016, a total of 2,55,708 refugees from Iran, Iraq, Libya, Somalia, Sudan, Syria, and Yemen have been admitted to the US since the start of 2008. Those countries account for almost 40 per cent of the 6,42,593 total refugees who have come to the US in that time period, according to the State Department's Refugee Processing Center.

Back home in India, after years of political stasis and a generalized state of drift and decline, 2014 heralded the assumption of the new government at the centre in India, one with an avowedly keen desire to power India—though not necessarily all Indians—into a different league of nations. By a quirk of fate and electoral arithmetic, the right-wing dispensation that came to power at the centre also—for the first time ever and against the run of history—came to share electoral and political power in Jammu and Kashmir. It was a political development hitherto unimaginable, one with far-reaching symbolism for the idea of a secular republic, and pregnant with new possibilities for the fragile mountain state that is also the crown of the country.

Rather unsurprisingly, but all too suddenly, the half-a-million-strong migrant Pandit community is back in favour, and their rehabilitation in Kashmir and restoration of their inalienable right to reclaim their homeland is at the centre of the governing agenda. Helpful noises have been heard, and repeated ad nauseum by India's prime minister, that a dignified return of the Pandits to their homeland is a top priority and a solemn commitment of the government at the centre. These solemn affirmations are seldom followed through with a roadmap of reconciliation between the minority Pandits and the majority Muslims that together constitute the demographic reality of Kashmir.

Small wonder then that the Pandits will stay out of Kashmir, homeless for a long, long time to come. To the extent that the return of the Pandits is tied to the larger idea of restoring and reinforcing the secular character of the state in one of India's most deeply polarized provinces, the idea of India will have to wait some more to realize its true spirit of equity, justice, and diversity.

By spawning a culture of 'packages' and economic freebies much like the benevolent monarchs of yore, those in the corridors of power, to use Einstein's deficiency of insanity, insist on doing the same thing in the same way over and over again, while hoping for a different result. Reconciliation demands, first and foremost, that truth be told and genuine redemption sought by the perpetrators and those complicit in the crime of standing by in silent helplessness when they were called upon to uphold the writ and rule of law, without fear or favour. For the Pandits to return to the land of their forebears after a quarter century of wanton homelessness, the basis of a new beginning will lie in the precept and the practice of a new social and political compact that is steeped in a genuine desire for atonement and fair play on the part of the state and the Muslim majority community. A sleight of hand will not work.

It will be a monumental mistake to seduce this demoralized community into returning to their homeland by luring them into generous freebies and financial incentives that play on their current economic vulnerabilities, without first cementing inter-communal trust and understanding among the dispossessed Pandits and the Muslims of Kashmir. Upholding truth is easier said than done when the polity is infested by a crisis of character and widespread venality. For India to stay united and one, Kashmir has to show the way.

Today or tomorrow, those in charge of the affairs of the state will have to bite the bullet by demonstrating a manifestly forceful and unambiguous desire to own their fair share of responsibility in being unable to stem, stop, and reverse the tide of violent extremism. By not coming to the rescue of the threatened and intimidated Pandits, these powers that be were almost complicit in fostering conditions for such a denouement through sustained dilution of the secular fabric of the Constitution of India by rank misgovernance and the practice of active religion-based discrimination against the Pandits for decades in the run up to the so-called 'exodus' of Pandits between December 1989 and March 1990.

My migration to Delhi happened a quarter of a century ago. In the end, we all learn to adapt in order to survive. I learnt it too. However, homesickness never left me even as I made myself at home in new places with the deft expertise that survival demands. Deep inside, I have missed the streets, smells, and the scenes that I was born into and shaped by. Hibernating through 25 long tropical summers, away from Kashmir, I have always felt as if I came to these new lands, agreed somehow to sleep over for a few days too many, but will go back to sleep in my own home one day. That thought never leaves me.

In the times that we find ourselves in, it will need a massive leap of faith to expect that politics in Kashmir is about to be cleansed of its deep sclerosis that has fed on massive injections of cash transferred from the Centre to buy peace with the Kashmiris—and the Kashmiri political class in the main—in favour of their silence on the core question of the political status of the state vis-à-vis the dominion of India. Blackmail begets more blackmail. And so it has been through the course of India's struggle over the last seven decades, to hold on to Kashmir through the cultivation of cliques and dynasts by dispensing power and pelf, instead of engagement and dialogue.

Engagement and dialogue. This, pretty much, ought to be the starting point of resolution of all conflicts that have led to an ever-rising tide of human migration all across the globe. The stories in the book stand witness that the way out of the cul-de-sac of displacement lies in the search for the right ideas for restoring respect and dignity to the growing multitudes of the displaced who, for the most part, find themselves in the maelstrom of someone else's making.

Acknowledgements

A rude realization of the sheer obscenity of an utterly devastated home came to me in 2014 in a desolate corner of the fully destroyed Old City of Homs in Syria. I ran into Suad, a young mother and widow—her husband having died from a stroke—who surveyed the aftermath of arson and looting, the merciless desecration of her home and possessions. Her eyes sad and face ashen, she was unable to put her feelings into words. A big thank you to Lana, my friend and colleague from the UNICEF office in Homs, who went with me to the fully destroyed site of the Old City after the siege to the city was lifted—a siege that had lasted well over a year and reduced the few hundred civilians who survived the siege to starving skeletons with sunken cheeks and vacuous eyes. The place resembled a burnt-down, vandalized, and derelict graveyard where once religions and cultures mingled and thrived and spoke to each other as only best friends can.

A big thank you to Razan Rashidi—super friend, super person, and the best UNICEF communications officer bar none in a conflict setting. Words can never be enough to express my appreciation for your shining intellect, and your swift, practical, and generous support at critical junctures when I was stuck for ideas to reach out to the war-ravaged and affected Syrian youth to contribute their stories, and to organize top-rate translation in double-quick time. I am in a debt of gratitude to Dalia Masri, who bravely accepted to take on the English translation of three of the most complex stories in the book that called for a deep and thorough understanding of literature and translation.

To Kinda Katranji, one of the wisest and warmest persons living in Damascus who opened my eyes to the many sights and scenes of Syria and went out of her way to arrange for my discussions with top Arabic language publishers in the Middle East. For all the long hours spent talking about the grief and glory of Syria, I can only say thank you.

In Ethiopia, Kisut Gebre Egziabher in the UNHCR helped open up my perspective on the refugees from South Sudan, Yemen, Eritrea, and the DRC, but also doors to Aweke Ayalew, the redoubtable and most helpful man in-charge of the Administration for Refugees and Returnee Affairs in Addis Ababa. To both these extraordinary gentlemen, my sincere appreciation and genuine thanks.

A big thank you is due to Hindu Singh Sodha, founder of Pak Visthapit Sangh and Seemant Lok Sangathan, and his genial colleague and fellow refugee from Pakistan, Ashok Suthar, for helping me connect with the deeply scarred and persecuted minorities across the border. I would like to thank UNDP's Anil Chandrika, Adrian Edwards in the UNHCR, and Edward Carwardine and Simon Ingram in UNICEF, for engaging with me in many constructive ways and their encouragement from time to time.

The book would be devoid of its geographically textured soul without the contributions by some of the finest practitioners of the craft of writing, blogging, and journalism. From India, Dr Kundan Lal Chowdhury and Dola Mitra; from Pakistan, Qaiser Khan Afridi; from Romania, Ioana Moldovan, from Australia, Melanie Groves; and from Syria, Mohammed, Naila, and Odai deserve my heartfelt gratitude for putting up with my persistent nagging and responding to my entreaties to contribute their respective stories on displaced humans they related to in India, Myanmar, Afghanistan, Ukraine, Tibet, and Syria. In the case of Ioana, she also shared liberally her invaluable and top-quality pictures from the frontlines of conflict in Ukraine.

To each one of the persons who talk to you directly through the pages of the book, I thank you for being convinced that your stories are worth telling and for the world, worth knowing about. In allowing me to talk to you and listen to your remarkable accounts of the journeys that you undertook and the storms you weathered and survived, you made me richer, better, and stronger as a person. I cannot thank you enough for being my fellow collaborators in this effort to let the world know that you exist.

I feel blessed to have been, until recently, a part of the United Nations, a privilege that entitled me to serve in several once-glorious countries now laid low by strife and violence. These assignments helped me to meet and interact with a plethora of men, women, and children of multiple ethnicities and nationalities, races, religions, and colours, and see up close how war and violence play out in these places and turn ordinary lives upside down, sometimes irretrievably. It would have taken many times more effort to be in these countries on my own at the height of the conflicts that they found themselves in.

My childhood buddy Rohit Das, a publishing industry veteran, provided me the initial confidence to reach out to some of the finest publishing houses with this manuscript. In the end, it took the editorial team at Oxford University Press to be convinced of the usefulness of this effort and for it to become a book. Thanks are due to the editorial team at OUP for their cheerful encouragement throughout this engagement, for their professional chaperoning of the project, and for their stupendous efforts in honing the manuscript and bringing it in the shape that you find it in your hands. My sincere appreciation is due to the design team at OUP for engaging with me from an early stage to conceptualize the cover that visually captures the theme of global human displacement.

Reena Mehta, the very talented communications specialist was an effective sounding board in the early days of the project when I was keen to bounce off my thinking about the right approach for this enterprise.

A sincere thank you is due to my friend Anita Anand who went through many versions of the draft and provided robust feedback on both the style and substance of the book.

The seeds for the book were planted in the fall of 2014 by my wife Sudha via an innocuous text message that called me to action, literally, because our own 25th year of internal displacement was around the corner (in 2015). A brief, long-distance exchange followed, and Sudha's wake-up call had crystallized itself into a nebulous idea of a book of stories that might just work. Soon, Tamanna, our daughter, was pulled into the conversation from faraway Blacksburg, Virginia. Tamanna made the project her own, pitching in with ideas, time, energy, creativity, passion, and determination throughout the nine months that it has taken to complete this labour of love. But for their limitless love and belief in me, this work would not have seen the light of day. The book is as much theirs as it is mine.

I owe it to the blessings of my parents and the best wishes of my extended family of friends, relatives and well-wishers—far too many to be named and just too special to me to be overlooked—that gave me the strength and confidence to take off on multiple journeys to conflict-affected places around the world.

And how can I forget Amma's love and affection, my most abiding source of inspiration when it comes to getting through life against all odds. Her genial and ever-assuring presence and a heart full of blessings has been a source of strength and inspiration, especially on days when I was assailed by self-doubt and low motivation.

About the Author

Kumar M. Tiku has served the United Nations (UN) in multiple conflict-affected countries. For over 15 years, his association with the United Nations Development Programme (UNDP) has taken him to Afghanistan, Sudan, Fiji, and Iraq, in addition to his work in India. Aside from UNDP, he served UNICEF in multiple roles, including as Chief of External Communications in Syria.

Kumar was born in Srinagar, in the Indian state of Jammu and Kashmir. In 1990, nearly half a million strong Kashmiri Pandit community that he belongs to was forced to flee its homeland en masse in the face of a wave of radical extremist militancy that has since engulfed the state. As a fair and just reconciliation defies the Kashmir imbroglio, he remains an unrecognized internally displaced person in India, a full quarter century after the migration of the minority Pandits from the valley of Kashmir, a homeland that they inhabited for over a thousand years and more.

About the Contributors

Dola Mitra is a Kolkata-based senior journalist, currently with *Outlook*, India's leading news weekly.

Melanie Groves is an aspiring development worker, inveterate writer and blogger, and an intrepid traveller.

Dr Kundan Lal Chowdhury is a practicing physician and poet and writer of many books on Kashmir and Kashmiris.

Qaiser Khan Afridi is a communications officer with the UNHCR in Pakistan.